THE WAY
PEOPLE
LIVE

Life in Ancient Greece

by Don Nardo

Lucent Books, P.O. Box 289011, San Diego, CA 92198-9011

Titles in The Way People Live series include:
Cowboys in the Old West
Life During the French Revolution
Life in Ancient Greece
Life in an Eskimo Village
Life in the Warsaw Ghetto
Life in War-Torn Bosnia
Life on a Medieval Pilgrimage
Life on an Israeli Kibbutz

Library of Congress Cataloging-in-Publication Data

Nardo, Don, 1947–
    Life in ancient Greece / by Don Nardo.
        p.   cm. — (The way people live)
    Includes bibliographical references and index.
    Summary: Account of daily life during the golden age of Greece.
    ISBN 1-56006-327-0 (alk. paper)
    1. Greece—Civilization—To 146 B.C.—Juvenile literature.
    2. Greece—Social life and customs—Juvenile literature. [1. Greece—
Civilization—To 146 B.C.   2. Greece—Social life and customs.]
    I. Title.   II. Series.
DF78.N37   1996
938—dc20   95–30504
                                                                     CIP
                                                                      AC

Contents

Discovering the Humanity in Us All

The Way People Live series focuses on pockets of human culture. Some of these are current cultures, like the Eskimos of the Arctic; others no longer exist, such as the Jewish ghetto in Warsaw during World War II. What many of these cultural pockets share, however, is the fact that they have been viewed before, but not completely understood.

To really understand any culture, it is necessary to strip the mind of the common notions we hold about groups of people. These stereotypes are the archenemies of learning. It does not even matter whether the stereotypes are positive or negative; they are confining and tight. Removing them is a challenge that's not easily met, as anyone who has ever tried it will admit. Ideas that do not fit into the templates we create are unwelcome visitors—ones we would prefer remain quietly in a corner or forgotten room.

The cowboy of the Old West is a good example of such confining roles. The cowboy was courageous, yet soft-spoken. His time (it is always a he, in our template) was spent alternatively saving a rancher's daughter from certain death on a runaway stagecoach, or shooting it out with rustlers. At times, of course, he was likely to get a little crazy in town after a trail drive, but for the most part, he was the epitome of inner strength. It is disconcerting to find out that the cowboy is human, even a bit childish. Can it really be true that cowboys would line up to help the cook on the trail drive grind coffee, just hoping he would give them a little stick of pep-permint candy that came with the coffee shipment? The idea of tough cowboys vying with one another to help "Coosie" (as they called their cooks) for a bit of candy seems silly and out of place.

So is the vision of Eskimos playing video games and watching MTV, living in prefab housing in the Arctic. It just does not fit with what "Eskimo" means. We are far more comfortable with snow igloos and whale blubber, harpoons and kayaks.

Although the cultures dealt with in Lucent's The Way People Live series are often historically and socially well known, the emphasis is on the personal aspects of life. Groups of people, while unquestionably affected by their politics and their governmental structures, are more than those institutions. How do people in a particular time and place educate their children? What do they eat? And how do they build their houses? What kinds of work do they do? What kinds of games do they enjoy? The answers to these questions bring these cultures to life. People's lives are revealed in the particulars and only by knowing the particulars can we understand these cultures' will to survive and their moments of weakness and greatness.

This is not to say that understanding politics does not help to understand a culture. There is no question that the Warsaw ghetto, for example, was a culture that was brought about by the politics and social ideas of Adolf Hitler and the Third Reich. But the Jews who were crowded together in the ghetto cannot be understood by the Reich's politics. Their life was a day-to-day battle for existence, and the creativity and methods they used to prolong their lives is a vital story of human perseverance that would be denied by focusing only on the institutions of Hitler's Germany. Knowing that children as young as five or six outwitted Nazi guards on a daily basis, that Jewish policemen helped the Germans control the ghetto, that children attended secret schools in the ghetto and even earned diplomas—these are the things that reveal the fabric of life, that can inspire, intrigue, and amaze.

Books in the The Way People Live series allow both the casual reader and the student to see humans as victims, heroes, and onlookers. And although humans act in ways that can fill us with feelings of sorrow and revulsion, it is important to remember that "hero," "predator," and "victim" are dangerous terms. Heaping undue pity or praise on people reduces them to objects, and strips them of their humanity.

Seeing the Jews of Warsaw only as victims is to deny their humanity. Seeing them only as they appear in surviving photos, staring at the camera with infinite sadness, is limiting, both to them and to those who want to understand them. To an object of pity, the only appropriate response becomes "Those poor creatures!" and that reduces both the quality of their struggle and the depth of their despair. No one is served by such two-dimensional views of people and their cultures.

With this in mind, the The Way People Live series strives to flesh out the traditional, two-dimensional views of people in various cultures and historical circumstances. Using a wide variety of primary quotations—the words not only of the politicians and government leaders, but of the real people whose lives are being examined—each book in the series attempts to show an honest and complete picture of a culture removed from our own by time or space.

By examining cultures in this way, the reader will notice not only the glaring differences from his or her own culture, but also will be struck by the similarities. For indeed, people share common needs—warmth, good company, stability, and affirmation from others. Ultimately, seeing how people really live, or have lived can only enrich our understanding of ourselves.

Striving for the Good Life

As was true of all other peoples in history, the ancient Greeks' everyday actions, habits, customs, and beliefs were motivated and guided by their general outlook on life. In examining the Greeks' lives, one is immediately struck by both the similarities and differences between their general outlook on life and our own. Like many people in modern developed countries such as the United States, the Greeks were vital, active, individualistic, and highly competitive. They wanted to get the best out of life, to feel useful and fulfilled, and to be happy.

In some ways, the "good life" then was the same as it is now. Like their modern counterparts, the Greeks valued good health and recognized it as an important prerequisite for a fulfilling, happy life. "Health," went the

Runners carrying shields sprint to the finish line in one of the Olympic footraces staged every four years at Olympia in southern Greece.

The city of Athens as it appeared in the second century A.D., *when Greece was part of the Roman Empire.*

words of a Greek hymn dating from about 400 B.C., "may I dwell with you for the rest of my days, and may you be kind and stay with me. For without you no man is happy."[1] Today's commercials and advertisements regularly equate good health with beauty, especially youthful beauty. Modern advertisers send the message that youth and good looks can help ensure a happy life. The Greeks would have responded well to such advertising, for they greatly admired beauty in all things, but most of all in the youthful human body. Classical historian C. M. Bowra comments:

> The belief in health passes imperceptibly into the belief in beauty, which is equally derived from the notion that through it men and women resemble the gods. . . . The beauty which they admired and celebrated with many statues of naked young men and well-clothed maidens was that of the body when it is passing into manhood or womanhood.[2]

The Greeks also valued personal wealth, knowing full well that while wealth might not guarantee happiness, it at least would ensure material comforts. These Greek values, along with their splendid arts, architecture, literature, and philosophy, have been passed down through the ages and are still engrained in modern Western societies. In many ways, indeed, as classical scholar Charles Gulick puts it, ancient Greece was "the germ and seed of all that is best in life today."[3]

Delight in Noble Actions

But some of the Greeks' most important everyday values did not survive the long journey through the ages in their entirety. Today, for instance, many people would say that a person who is healthy, strong, beautiful, and wealthy has most of the basic ingredients of the good life. But these attributes are only part of what the Greeks saw as necessary for enjoying the good life. The Greeks separated life's "goods" into two broad categories—physical goods and spiritual goods. Of the physical goods, the fourth-century philosopher Plato wrote, "the first is health, the second beauty, the third strength, and the fourth wealth."[4]

At least as important as these physical goods, and perhaps more so, was delighting in "noble actions," stated Plato's famous pupil, the philosopher Aristotle. The Greeks held that what made a person noble was virtue, or spiritual good, and they recognized four major virtues: courage, temperance, justice, and wisdom. The goal was to have and

An Unprecedented Creature

An essential part of the ancient Greeks' general outlook on life, a view that directly affected their everyday religious, social, and political customs, was their strong belief that "man" was an especially worthy being. (Their frequent use of the word "man" was usually not intended to refer to males only, but rather, referred to humanity in general.) The noted historian C. M. Bowra wrote in The Greek Experience:

"They saw that man was indeed an unprecedented creature, worthy of awe and wonder in the scale of his inventions and his enterprises. . . . Just as everything serves some purpose or other, so man serves a purpose in the scheme of things and realizes his full nature in it. This is to develop his *arete*, or inborn capacities, so far as he possibly can. . . . It is assumed as beyond dispute that man has such an end and that it is fine and noble."

utilize all four virtues, and they believed that the lack of even one virtue detracted from the others.

The first virtue to strive for, courage, meant more than just bravery in battle. It was also the fortitude to stand up for what one thought was right, even against formidable odds. The Greeks defined temperance as a kind of polite restraint; that is, performing everyday actions without vulgar display or arrogance. In fact, they found arrogant attitudes and displays, what they called *hybris*, both shocking and distasteful. They also had a strong sense of justice, especially regarding the civil rights of the individual, which was noticeably absent from most other ancient societies. The fifth-century B.C. Athenian playwright Euripides summed up the general view, saying that a good man was he who brought no evil upon his townsmen nor upon himself by denying justice to others.

A Unique View of the Human Being

Of all the spiritual goods, the Greeks admired wisdom, or *sophia*, most of all. "To think is the greatest virtue," wrote the philosopher-scientist Heraclitus in 500 B.C., "and wisdom consists of speaking what is true and acting in obedience to nature."[5] The Greeks believed that wisdom was good, not just for the material advantages it could bring someone, but in and of itself. They developed almost a reverence for knowledge, truth, and the constant pursuit of both. In ancient Greece, in contrast to most other societies, including today's, philosophers and other intellectuals were just as famous, respected, and honored as great athletes and warriors.

The ancient Greeks' strong preoccupation with the concepts of temperance, justice,

This painting depicts a Greek teacher, possibly the philosopher Socrates, preparing to give a lecture in a crowded hall.

and wisdom as prerequisites of the good life set them apart from others. It also colored everything they did. From their adherence to temperance came the serene, restrained majesty of their architecture and sculpture. From their love of justice were born the concepts of individual worth and of political democracy. And from their worship of wisdom and truth came the great dramatic and philosophical works that helped to shape the development of Western thought.

And overriding their vision of the physical and spiritual virtues that made life good, happy, and worth living was their unique view of the human being in the general scheme of things. Humans, as they saw it, held a special place in the natural order. The Greeks did not, as so many other peoples have, see people as being corrupt and sinful by nature, but rather, as inherently worthy, endowed with a huge potential for useful and beneficial thought and action. This was a view of enormous energy and optimism that made each new year of life something to look forward to. The great Athenian playwright Sophocles captured this unique outlook in a single phrase. "Wonders are there many," he wrote, "but none more wonderful than man himself."[6]

Citizens and Slaves: The People of the Greek City-State

Greece is a warm, dry, and mountainous land about the size of New York State. Its rugged, often cliff-lined coast and many beautiful offshore islands rim the western and southern waters of the warm, intensely blue Aegean Sea, an inlet of the larger Mediterranean Sea. Today, Greece is one of Europe's poorest and least influential countries. But in ancient times, the Greek mainland and islands were the home of one of the most culturally splendid and influential civilizations in world history. The ancient Greeks, who called their land Hellas and themselves Hellenes, left behind a magnifi-cent cultural heritage of art, government, and ideas that helped to shape later Western, or European-based, lands and peoples. Many of our common social customs and habits, artis-tic styles, political concepts, and vocabulary words originated in everyday life in ancient Greek society.

Greece's Distinct Ages

Greek civilization lasted for more than two thousand years, and historians have conve-niently divided that long span into four dis-

Overlooking the rugged, island-studded Aegean coast, the ruins of an ancient temple stand silently and serenely in the midday sun.

A reconstruction of the Athenian Acropolis as it appeared at the height of its magnificence in the fifth and fourth centuries B.C., *the so-called Classic Age of Greece.*

tinct periods or ages. The earliest period, lasting from about 3000 to 1100 B.C., is variously referred to as the Greek Bronze Age, the Minoan period, and the Age of Heroes. During these years two early Greek peoples—the Minoans and their imitators and eventual successors, the Mycenaeans—built a sophisticated culture on the Greek islands and in many parts of mainland Greece. Writes scholar Rodney Castleden:

> The Minoans were above all creative and original people, fiercely life-affirming and devoted to the worship of their many goddesses and gods. From the evidence so far gathered, their attention was finely divided between economic production, trade . . . [and] their material well-being on the one hand, and devotion to a complex and demanding religious creed . . . on the other. There are great gaps in our knowledge of the Minoans, and we have

to be able to modify our view of them in the light of new . . . discoveries. Minoan archaeology is still excitingly young and we can be sure that many new and unexpected things remain to be learned about this remarkable civilization.[7]

The Minoan/Mycenaean culture ended abruptly about 1100 B.C. when the Dorians, a warlike people from extreme northern Greece, swept down and destroyed the southern fortresses and towns. Greece then entered a cultural dark age, lasting for about three hundred years, about which little of any certainty is known. What *is* certain is that during the dark age new political units known as city-states, or poleis, began to evolve separately on islands and in sheltered valleys. Most typically, each polis consisted of a central town surrounded by small villages and farmland. Most of the central towns were built around a hill or cliff called an acropolis, which means "high place of the city" in Greek. The inhabitants of a polis fortified their acropolis to defend against attackers in times of war. Although most such towns were physically similar, they evolved differing traditions and governments and came to think of themselves as separate, tiny nations.

As many poleis became increasingly prosperous and powerful, Greece rose from its dark age into what historians call the Archaic Age, lasting from about 800 to 500 B.C. For many city-states, this was a time of growing trade, the establishment of colonies along the shores of the Aegean, Black, and Mediterranean Seas, and much political experimentation. By the end of the Archaic Age, two poleis had emerged as the most powerful and influential in Greece. These were Athens, located on the Attic peninsula on the eastern coast, and Sparta, in the southern part of the Peloponnesus, the large peninsula that makes up southern Greece.

The following two centuries, from about 500 to 300 B.C., in which Greece, dominated primarily by Athens and Sparta, reached its pinnacle of power and high culture, are referred to as the Classic Age. Sparta developed a rigid military system and the strongest, most feared army in all of Greece. Its peculiar and very strict customs and traditions were not typical of those of most other poleis. Athens, on the other hand, was Greece's cultural and political leader. It was Athens that erected public buildings and sculptures at which travelers marveled and that was the first to experiment with democracy. C. M. Bowra writes:

No other Greek state can be compared with her for the range, strength, and originality of her achievement, and indeed . . . she presents the culmination of the many forces that . . . made the Greeks unique

among peoples and [gave] a special character to their outlook and their habits. . . . She embodied all that was worth having in the civilization of Greece.[8]

For this reason, many other city-states adopted or copied Athenian customs and ideas and looked to Athens for guidance and leadership. Recognizing this leadership role, Athens's famed democratic leader Pericles remarked, "I say that the whole city is an education for Greece."[9] Thus, examining everyday life in Athens gives a fair approximation of everyday life in most of the rest of Greece in the Classic Age.

The Social Pyramid

The basic social structure of Athens, for instance, was certainly typical of those of other city-states. Classical Greek society was built upon a series of interlocking social units, the origins of which stretched back into the obscure and little-known times before the Archaic Age. The most basic social unit was the family, or *oikos* (the plural is *oikoi*). A typical *oikos* consisted of an extended household group, including parents, children, grandparents, and the servants and slaves who were dependent on the head of the household. The head of the household was almost always a free adult male and the position traditionally passed from father to son.

When the head of a family had more than one son, the sons eventually established their own *oikoi*, which remained linked to the parent family through kinship ties. This was the basis of the next largest social group, the clan, or *genos* (the plural is *gene*). According to historian Michael Grant, a *genos* "consisted of a group of families (or perhaps in some cases of a single large family, including adult sons and

An ancient sculpture shows the members of a Greek family. The father, the family head, reaches into a basket held by a slave.

the members of a phratry were related by blood. The exceptions to this rule were people who, because of various circumstances, had no family or clan. A phratry could and often did adopt, or include, these unfortunate individuals into its ranks.

Reorganizing Attica

The tribe, or *phylai*, the largest single social unit, commonly consisted of three phratries. Athens had four traditional tribes, while other poleis had varying numbers of tribes. In the late sixth century B.C., the democratic leader Cleisthenes reshaped Athenian tribal structure. As the ancient Greek historian Herodotus described it, he

> changed the number of Athenian tribes from four to ten, and abolished the old names. . . . He named the new tribes after heroes [mythical warriors remembered from the Age of Heroes] . . . appointing ten [tribal] presidents—*phylarchs*—instead of the original four.[11]

Cleisthenes also divided the Athenian territory of Attica into about 140 small geographical units, or communities, called demes (*demois*). These eventually became the focus of the social and religious activities of the clans and phratries. One reason for this social reorganization was to create a more reliable military force. Before, each tribe had provided an unspecified number of soldiers for the army on a more or less voluntary basis. Under the new plan, each of the ten tribes was required to supply a minimum number of troops during a military emergency. This ensured an army that was both larger and drawn more fairly and evenly from all quarters of society.

their wives), which claimed descent from a common ancestor."[10] The heads of these *gene* eventually became more important and influential than the heads of individual households in the affairs of the extended family. It was common, for example, for the head of a clan to arrange marriages for his various sons, daughters, nephews, nieces, cousins, and grandchildren, all from various *oikoi*.

The next units in the widening social pyramid were the phratry and the tribe, both highly extended kinship groups. The typical phratry, or "blood brotherhood," consisted of about thirty clans, about as many people as lived in a small Greek village. And indeed, many villages or city neighborhoods were dominated by one or two phratries. The phratry, often the central focus of social gatherings and religious rituals, was similar to a modern religious congregation, except that

What's in a Name?

To Shakespeare's famous question, What's in a name?, an ancient Greek would undoubtedly answer, A great deal! In naming children, parents in Athens and other Greek poleis did not choose randomly or try to find first names that sounded pleasing when matched with surnames, or family names. In Greece, explains classical scholar Charles Gulick in his book Modern Traits in Old Greek Life:

"Names always bore an intelligible meaning and were of good omen [foretold possible success in life]. Their [meanings] could be recognized, in almost all cases, as soon as the name was pronounced. Thus Pericles is 'he of exceeding glory'; Sophocles, 'of glorious wisdom.'. . . The meaning of our [modern] surnames is understood now only by the philologist [language expert]. . . . But with the Greeks the meaning of proper names was still consciously felt. . . . The name of an Athenian child, as registered by the father in the records of his brotherhood [phratry] and deme [local community], would read, for example, 'Socrates, son of Sophroniscus, of the deme Alopeke.' There were no family names in this early society, although it was sometimes the practice to give boys of the same family names compounded of similar elements, such as Demosthenes, Demomeles, and Demotimus, all kinsmen. The oldest male child commonly received the name of his paternal grandfather."

Citizen-Militia Versus Standing Army

Military service was one of the principal duties of male Athenians. When a young Athenian man reached the age of eighteen, he entered a military training corps called the *Epheboi*. After two years of general training, he recited publicly a loyalty oath to the polis that stated in part:

> I will not disgrace my sacred weapons nor desert the comrade at my side. . . . I will hand on my fatherland greater and better than I found it. I will obey the magistrates [government officials] and the existing laws. . . . I will honor the temples and the religion which my forefathers established.[12]

After taking this oath, the young man was thereafter a full-fledged hoplite, a heavily armored infantry soldier who fought with a six-foot-long spear and a short sword. The term hoplite was derived from the *hoplon*, the round shield of wood and bronze an infantryman carried. In Athens and most other poleis, hoplites were mainly citizen-militia between the ages of twenty and sixty who could be called upon to fight at any time.

The major exception to this arrangement was the unusually strict military establishment in Sparta. To develop and maintain the renowned discipline and fighting prowess of their army, the Spartans developed the *agoge*, a rigid and harsh system of military practices and institutions. This system became so far-reaching and ingrained in Spartan society that it had a profound effect on almost every aspect of Spartan daily life, commencing from the very moment of birth. In the first phase of the *agoge*, a group of town elders examined all male babies. If they

This bas-relief, or partially raised sculpture, shows two Greek soldiers with their round hoplons, *but without their armor.*

considered a child too weak, they ordered him "exposed," or left outside on a mountain-side to die. If deemed strong enough, the child lived to face later stages of the *agoge.* Describing these, classical scholar C. E. Robinson writes:

> At [the age of] seven home-life ended, and the boy was drafted into a sort of boarding-school with sixty or more others. . . . All lived and fed together . . . and it was part of their training that the boys should supplement their scanty rations by stealing off the neighboring farms. This practice was intended to develop resourcefulness and courage. . . . Tough-ness was, indeed, the principal quality

which the [Spartan] system aimed at pro-ducing. The boys went barefoot, wore but a single garment, and lay on a bed of . . . reeds.[13]

The young Spartan trainees were also forced to swim in ice-cold rivers and to engage in rough, often brutal sports. Typical was a game in which a team of boys stood on an island in the midst of a stream. Another team had to push them off the island using whatever means necessary, including savage kicking, biting, and eye gouging.

As adults, the Spartan hoplites, who con-stituted a full-time standing army rather than a part-time militia, continued their harsh reg-imen. They lived in communal barracks with-out comforts or decoration, wore plain cloth-

A Spartan elder examines a male infant to determine whether he is strong or weak. Weak babies were left outside to die.

ing, and ate a few simple foods—mainly bread, cheese, and pork. Such frugal and austere conditions have been called "spartan" ever since. But though harsh, Sparta's military system had the desired effect. It produced, says Michael Grant, quiet, obedient, and "ruthless young men [who], aiming at the single end of the national interest and survival, [were] for a long time, [by] far the best soldiers in Greece."[14]

Greek Women

Military service was only one of the duties and privileges of citizenship in Greece. Citizens, of course, were allowed to participate to one degree or another in government. But because the Greek poleis, like most other ancient societies, defined citizenship rather narrowly, only a minority of the population could either vote or hold public office. In Sparta, for example, only free adult males born of Spartan families were considered citizens, or "Spartiates." And in Athens, only free adult males born in Athenian territory, that is, Attica, were citizens who could take part in government.

Though Athenian women were considered citizens, too, they fell into a special citizenship category, the *astoi*, who lacked civic privileges. Grant points out that women's

only civic role consisted of giving birth to citizens, but this made them citizens of a kind themselves. . . . Their status as wives and mothers could never be wholly degraded without degrading their husbands and sons. Women could only achieve anything through men.[15]

Debating Women's Equality

The idea that men were superior to and should therefore dominate women was generally accepted as a fact of nature or the will of the gods in ancient Greece. However, some prominent Greek thinkers did not fully agree with this concept, and they often debated the issue in intellectual circles. Plato, for example, agreed that men were, morally speaking, better than women, writing in his *Laws*, "Woman's nature is inferior to that of men in capacity of virtue." Yet he added in his *Republic*, "At the same time many women are in many things superior to many men." Plato advocated that, while women, being weaker and less virtuous, were not exactly equal to men, they could still perform many duties as well as men if given the chance. Therefore, society should at least give women equal opportunity to succeed. "If women are to have the same duties as men," he wrote, "they must have the same education."

Aristotle disagreed with his teacher, Plato, and staunchly supported the traditional, conservative view. Women, he said, were obviously physically, socially, and morally inferior to men, and marriages were friendships between unequals. "The female," Aristotle wrote in his *History of Animals*, "is more disheartened, depressed, insolent, and more given to lying, than the male. She is likewise more easily deceived." Therefore, women should be controlled and guided by men. Unfortunately for most Greek women, most Greek men agreed with Aristotle's view.

Greek women converse while engaging in routine household duties. The woman kneeling by the laundry basket is a household slave.

In fact, most Greek women led quiet, sheltered, and often secluded lives and lived in the shadows of their fathers, husbands, and grown sons. This biased arrangement was justified partly on the grounds that it protected the "weaker" gender, especially younger, more innocent women, from harm. As Charles Gulick explains:

Marriageable girls were surrounded with many safeguards which would be held intolerable today, and they saw their future husbands only at religious processions and sacrifices. Their seclusion may be explained in part by the great influx of foreigners into Athens in the Periclean Age [mid–fifth century B.C.], since conservative parents would be loath [very reluctant] to expose their daughters to contact with aliens, most of whom were of the lower classes. Rarely was the right of intermarriage accorded to an alien.[16]

As a rule, Greek women spent most of their time at home. They were allowed to go to market and to attend the theater and religious festivals, but only when accompanied by a male relative or family servant. Typical women's duties included managing the household slaves, making and mending clothes, weaving and spinning the wool for such garments, and overseeing the preparations for banquets and parties. A mother or wife usually had considerable authority over day-to-day household matters. About other, more "manly" matters, especially politics, she was expected to remain silent. "For women silence is a grace," wrote Sophocles.[17]

Other famous Greek men echoed this refrain. The statesman Pericles was progressive in politics and other areas yet displayed the typical male attitude of the time when he told a group of widowed Athenian mothers and wives, "Your greatest glory is not to be inferior to what God has made you, and the greatest glory of a woman is to be least talked about by men, whether they are praising you or criticizing you."[18]

There were some notable exceptions to this general subservient role of women. In Athens and many other city-states, a small class of women known as *hetairai*, or "companions," held a special status. They were, in essence, high-class prostitutes who provided men not only with sex, but also with entertainment and stimulating conversation. The *hetairai*, usually foreigners and therefore noncitizens, were often skilled musicians and dancers and much better educated than sheltered "respectable" Greek women.

Spartan women constituted another exception to the rule. Though they could not take part in government, they enjoyed more independence and authority in everyday life than women in the rest of Greece. This probably stemmed from the harsh military ethic of the *agoge*. For example, so that they might bear healthier, stronger sons for the army, Spartan women were encouraged to train for and compete in rigorous sports, a custom that Greeks in other poleis found shocking. And a Spartan mother was expected to punish, and even to kill, her sons for showing signs of cowardice.

Foreigners, Slaves, and Serfs

In addition to women, other large groups of people in Greek society were not accorded the right to vote or to hold public office. Among these were foreigners, either non-Greeks or natives of other Greek poleis. In Athens, these foreigners were called *metoikoi*, or metics. They were mostly merchants or tradespeople such as metalsmiths, potters, and jewelers. Although they played no role in government and could not own land or houses, metics made important contributions to the community. They provided products and services, paid taxes, and served as hoplites in the army. The Spartan version of the metics were the *perioikoi*, which meant "neighbors" or "dwellers round about." The *perioikoi* were considered inferi-

or to the Spartiates and, therefore, lived in their own villages. They engaged, writes Michael Grant,

> in commerce, industry, and navigation, as Spartiates did not. And in due course they also came to serve in the hoplite phalanx [military unit or formation], though even this did not entitle them to become equals [to the Spartiates].[19]

Another group lacking political rights, and most other rights for that matter, were the slaves. Most Greek slaves acquired their status by being born the children of slaves or by capture and enslavement during war. Like other ancient peoples, the Greeks accepted the idea of slavery as a natural fact of life. Aristotle described slaves as the best, most manageable, and most necessary property a man could own, and Herodotus declared that slavery was the will of the gods. Because this prevailing view of slaves applied mainly to foreigners, who most Greeks believed were less civilized than themselves, the idea of Greeks enslaving other Greeks was generally discouraged.

Slaves were an integral component of the Greek social structure. They did most of the manual labor, thus freeing citizens to pursue politics, the arts, and other intellectual and leisure endeavors. It is difficult to determine the number of slaves in any one family or polis at any given date. But many historians estimate that fifth-century B.C. Athens had 80,000 to 100,000 slaves, about a third of the population. A family of moderate means probably had 2 or 3 slaves, while a well-to-do citizen kept perhaps 15 to 20. Businesses and craft shops had even more slaves. An Athenian metic named Cephalus, for instance, supposedly used about 120 slaves in his prosperous shield-making shop.

For the most part, Greek slaves were well treated, often becoming trusted and cherished members of the families that owned them. Although some owners routinely smacked and flogged their slaves, the law usually prevented severe brutality. Comments C. E. Robinson:

> It was not permitted to put a slave to death. Unprovoked assault [on a slave] laid the assailant open to prosecution. . . . The slaves at Athens were anything but cringing creatures. They would even elbow passers-by out of their way in the street; and the trouble was that it was unsafe to punch their heads; for in dress and appearance they were so like freeborn citizens that it was quite easy to make a mistake.[20]

Slaves often received small wages that they could either spend or save to buy their freedom. A slave might also gain freedom from a kind master as a reward for long years of faithful service. The few slaves who did become such "freedmen" enjoyed the status of metics, and a handful of former slaves even became successful and wealthy. The most famous of these was Pasion, who was the richest banker and manufacturer in Athens when he died in 370 B.C. According to Grant:

> He began his career as a slave with a banking firm, becoming a freedman and later an Athenian citizen. He derived a large income from his bank and shield-workshop, enjoyed credit at all Greek commercial centers, and left [behind

In a Greek marketplace, a merchant conducts a slave auction of three recently captured war prisoners.

Aristotle was not alone in worrying that Athenian democracy was too liberal and might allow the poor and uneducated to dominate "more worthy" citizens. In an ancient document titled The Constitution of the Athenians, *a nameless individual, now routinely referred to as the "Old Oligarch," harshly criticized Athens's new democratic "constitution," or set of laws and political practices.*

"I do not at all approve of their having chosen this form of constitution because . . . they have given the advantages to the vulgar people at the cost of the good. . . . They everywhere give the vulgar and the poor and the common people the preference to the aristocrats. . . . When the poor, the people of small means, and the low individuals are prospering and their number is increasing, they will strengthen the democracy. . . . In every country [in which] the aristocracy is contrasted to the democracy, there being in the best people [aristocrats] the least immorality and wickedness, but the keenest eyes for morals; in the people on the other hand we find a very high degree of ignorance, disorder, and vileness; for poverty more and more leads them in the direction of bad morals, thus also the absence of education and in the case of some persons the ignorance which is due to the want [lack] of money."

when he died] extensive real estate and capital [money].[21]

The less common and darker side of Greek slavery was the treatment of the slaves who toiled in the mines, particularly the Athenian silver mines at Laureum in southern Attica. These workers were shackled in chains day and night, treated brutally, and had no hope of ever gaining their freedom. Only the most unruly and disobedient slaves, those considered unfit for domestic service, were sent to the mines, an assignment looked upon as a certain death sentence.

The treatment of the Spartan helots was also harsh. They were not slaves in the strictest sense, but rather serfs, or poor peasants forced to work the land in exchange for a small share of the harvest. The helots outnumbered the Spartiates by a factor of at least ten to one. To keep this valuable but potentially dangerous workforce in line,

Spartan citizens closely oversaw and regulated the helots and treated them in a cruel and inhumane manner. For example, it was a common and accepted right of passage for a young Spartiate military trainee to secretly stalk and kill one or more helots before becoming a hoplite.

Differing Political Systems

Perhaps a major reason why the classical Greeks excluded so many sectors of society from full citizenship and the privilege of taking part in politics was the unusual nature of their government. Kings and other absolute monarchs ruled in nearly every other land. Their word was law, and they granted minimal political authority and a few civil rights to only a handful of well-to-do nobles. In the Greek poleis, by contrast, most free males had extensive civil rights. Some poleis, following Athens's lead, even conducted their own experiments in democracy, a word made up of the Greek terms *demos*, "people," and *kratos*, "rule." Having gained political power and civil rights, Greek men did not want to risk losing their gains. They feared that sharing power with women and other social groups might limit their own power in government and lead to social chaos. In their view, some democracy was good but too much was dangerous. Aristotle, for example, liked many democratic principles, such as free speech, but believed that democracy, as a working political system, was flawed. He warned against the poor and other "unfit" groups gaining too much say in government. "A democracy," he said, "is a government in the hands of men of low birth, poverty, and vulgar employments."[22]

Full-blown democracy did not appear suddenly, nor was it the only form of government in Greece. During Greece's dark age and early Archaic Age, the Greek city-states were ruled by kings. But over the years an increasingly larger proportion of the male population gained civil freedoms and a voice in government. After overthrowing their kings, groups of prominent citizens often shared power in ruling councils, a system the Greeks called oligarchy, or "rule of the few." These oligarchs were always wealthy aristocrats, a word derived from the Greek term *aristoi*, meaning "best people."

Some poleis retained these systems well into the Classic Age. For instance Thebes, located a few miles north of Attica, and Corinth, in the northeastern Peloponnesus, maintained oligarchies run by aristocrats whose power was based on wealth, especially land ownership. But though not chosen by the people in democratic fashion, most of these oligarchs tended to be liberal rulers who listened to a wide range of advisers and community spokespeople and allowed considerable freedom of speech and expression. Sparta was governed by what Aristotle described as a mixture of monarchy, oligarchy, and democracy. The polis had two kings who ruled jointly and whose duties were to lead the armies and supervise religious rituals. Five *ephors*, or "overseers," administrated the day-to-day affairs of state. The *ephors* were elected annually by the *apella*, an assembly composed of all Spartiates over the age of thirty.

Democracy in Athens

In many other poleis, however, political reformers were bolder. They followed the Athenian lead by discarding their oligarchies and establishing varying degrees of democracy, although none went as far or were as suc-

This later Roman cameo of the Athenian teacher and writer Aristotle incorrectly depicts him without a full beard, the style that all men of his time followed.

cessful as Athens. Athens had a two-part legislature composed of the *Ecclesia*, or Assembly, and the *Boule*, or Council. The Council consisted of five hundred members, fifty from each tribe. Chosen annually by lot, or random drawing, they met in a building called the Tholos and formulated laws and state policies. The members of the Assembly then discussed and voted either to accept or to reject this legislation. The Assembly also elected new leaders each year. These included nine administrators, the archons, to run the government and ten military generals, the *strategoi*, to lead the armies and implement the foreign policy created by the legislature. According to scholars Susan Peach and Anne Millard:

> Every citizen had the right to speak and to vote at the Assembly, which met about once every ten days on a hill called the

Pnyx [near the Acropolis]. At least 6,000 citizens had to be present for a meeting to take place. If too few people attended, special police were sent out to round up more citizens.[23]

When these police found citizens shirking their civic duty, they swatted them with a rope dipped in red paint. Any man with a red stain on his tunic had to pay a fine to the state.

Athenian citizens were also expected to participate in the state's legal system by serving as jurors. A typical jury had from two hundred to four hundred members, partly to ensure that no significant number of them could be bribed or intimidated. C. E. Robinson remarks:

> To the quick-witted Athenians the chance of hearing a good . . . argument was a form of intellectual entertainment.

An orator waves his arms in an attempt to emphasize his point during a speech before the Athenian Assembly, which met near the summit of the Pnyx Hill.

There was therefore no [hesitation] to serve on the panel. Moreover, jurors were paid a small fee for their trouble; and a large number of candidates . . . were always waiting round the court doors in the morning.[24]

There were no judges or lawyers. Citizens presented their own cases before the juries and often hired professional speechwriters to help make their arguments sound more polished and convincing. When accused persons were found guilty, common penalties included fines and temporary loss of citizenship for minor offenses and exile or death for serious crimes.

The Momentous Awakening

The Athenian democracy featured another, specialized form of exile, the purpose of which was to remove unpopular, dishonest, or power-hungry leaders. This was the process of ostracism, in which citizens wrote the name of a person they wanted removed on pottery fragments called *ostrakons*. If the person received six thousand or more of these negative votes, he was banished from the polis for a period of ten years. As Michael Grant points out:

The exile of a tiresome politician would effectively silence him; for Athenian civilization was still mainly oral [built on person-to-person contact], and in an oral culture if you remove a man physically he has lost his lines of communication, and can no longer make trouble.[25]

Strong, decisive democratic features such as ostracism could not justify or excuse the far less equitable aspects of the governments of Athens and other Greek democracies. That so small a segment of the population could vote or hold office and that women and slaves had no say in shaping the policies and institutions that controlled them was certainly unfair by today's standards. But at the time, Greek democracy, despite its faults, marked a momentous awakening. It was the birth of a unique form of government, one that profoundly affected everyday lives and institutions. In its day, said historian Pierre Léveque, it was "the most advanced political system in the . . . world. This was the first time that a people was permitted to chart its own destiny, accepting as its highest authority the will of the majority."[26] In the fullness of time, modern nations such as the United States would embrace the democratic principles born in ancient Greece and go on to transform the world.

Country Versus City: Contrasting but Interdependent Lifestyles

The typical ancient Greek city-state featured two highly distinct living spheres, each of which supported its own separate customs and lifestyles. The first was the rural farm and village, where life tended to be quiet and slow paced and values were conservative. The other was the urban city or central town, the heart of the polis, known for its excitement, hustle and bustle, and more liberal attitudes. The contrast between Greek country and city was even greater than in modern societies, partly because the physical boundary between these spheres was so distinct. Most modern cities and towns thin out gradually, with suburban houses and shopping malls forming buffers between urban and rural areas. By contrast, most ancient cities ended very abruptly, often at imposing defensive city walls. When people traveled past the city limits, they passed immediately from congested urban streets into the quiet countryside. In Greece, that countryside most often consisted of rugged hills and gulleys dotted with farms and occasional villages. Many villages were no more than a few crude stone or wooden huts clustered around a single dirt road.

Contrasting Lifestyles

Not surprisingly, people who spent most of their time in one sphere or the other developed their own habits and views and often looked upon unfamiliar ways with a critical eye. The inhabitants of cities tended to believe that their rural neighbors were slow witted, miserly, old-fashioned, and superstitious. Farmers, on the other hand, viewed townspeople as lazy, insensitive, fast living spendthrifts. Greek comic playwrights derived a good deal of humor from such stereotypes. Typical was this speech from Aristophanes' *Clouds*, in which a former farmer bemoans having married a city girl:

> My life on the farm was the sweetest ever, untidy unswept, unbottoned [loose and easygoing], brimming with honey and sheep and oil, and then I married . . . a town lady, proud, luxurious, extravagant. Rare bedfellows! I reeking of wine vat, figs, and fleeces, she of perfume . . . and wanton kisses. . . . I used to tell her . . . *Wife, you drive too hard* [live too fast].[27]

But despite the many differences between country and city, the two were solidly linked and depended on each another. Farming was the mainstay of the Greek economy partly because wealth was mostly based on land ownership and exploitation. The well-to-do leaders of the polis, who lived mostly in fine urban townhouses, maintained their city lifestyles with revenues from their lands, usually overseen by employees called

An ancient vase painting depicts a typical scene from Greek country life, including hogs and a farmhand carrying water containers made of animal skin.

bailiffs. Also, the countryside supplied the city with most of its food. On the flip side of the relationship, the cities and towns housed the markets at which the farmers sold most of their crops. Thus, the polis was like a single coin with country life and city life anchored firmly on its opposing faces.

Country and city also shared and had to adapt to a fundamental and ever-present reality of Greek life—the weather. Greece has short, mild winters, sparse rainfall, and is for the most part extremely hot and arid. C. E. Robinson offers this colorful description of a typical Greek day:

> During spring, summer, and autumn cloudless skies last day after day. Dawn rises fresh and cool, with an invigorating [healthy] sparkle in the air giving a sense as of clear spring water. But long before noon the sun is scorching hot and the whole countryside athirst. Lizards creep out of the wall crannies to bask; crickets chirrup loudly among the grasses; and underfoot the dust lies inches deep. The afternoon wanes and then the sun goes down in a glory of molten gold.[28]

This hot but largely even and pleasant climate favored and supported an outside and open-air lifestyle. Farmers worked all day mainly outside, of course. Likewise, urban dwellers had their open-air markets, roofless theaters, and meeting places. Consequently, country and city dwellers alike spent most of their time outside the home (the exception being the more secluded lives of wives and mothers). The climate actually helped create a familiar, very congenial community atmosphere. Greek men who stayed inside too much were considered antisocial stick-in-the-muds. And because the average polis had a relatively small population, most people, whether in country or city, recognized, greet-

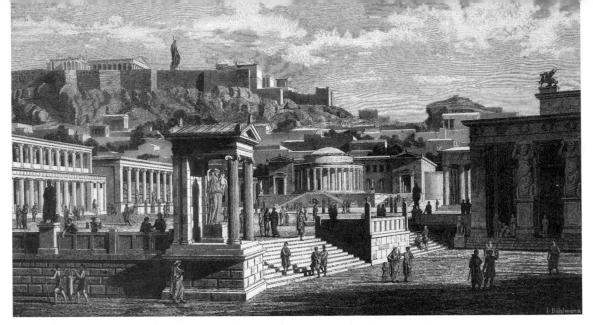

The agora, or marketplace, at Athens, as it probably appeared in the Classic Age. At left is the column-lined Stoa and rising in the background is the famed Acropolis.

ed, and conversed with their neighbors on a regular basis. Aristotle's remark that "those nations that dwell in warm climates have a longer life" may have been an exaggeration, but Greece was certainly one place where a warm climate bred a more sociable life.[29]

Working the Land

Greece's arid climate affected the character of everyday life in other ways. A prime example is the way the hot, dry weather, combined with the country's rocky terrain, shaped the very nature of farming. Over three-quarters of Greece is mountainous and unsuited to most agriculture. Only the small coastal plains and a few scattered inland areas are arable, and most of these areas have poor-quality soil. Olives, grapes, and figs can thrive in such conditions and became some of the principal crops. Corn and grains, mostly wheat and barley, grew less well and large

grain fields existed in only a few fertile plains, most notably in Thessaly, in north-central Greece, where rainfall was a little more plentiful. Because bread was a mainstay of the Greek diet, many poleis, especially larger ones like Athens, had to import their grain. For centuries, Athens spent much money and energy and even fought battles to maintain its life-giving grain connection to the fertile farmlands rimming the Black Sea.

Greek farmers learned the best times to plant and harvest their crops and scheduled their lives around these activities. In his *Works and Days*, probably dating from about 700 B.C., Hesiod, one of Greece's earliest and most respected writers, gave this advice to farmers:

At the first moment when the plowing season appears . . . set hard to work, your servants, yourself, everybody together plowing through wet weather and dry in the plowing season; rise early and drive the work along, so your fields will be full. Plow fallow [unplanted] in spring. . . . Do as I tell you, and the ears [of corn] will sweep the ground in their ripeness . . . and you can knock the spider-webs from your bins, and . . . be happy as you draw on all that substance that's stored up.[30]

As a rule farmers sowed their grain in October, in order to take advantage of the short winter rainy season. One man steered a wooden plow pulled by oxen or mules while a companion followed along tossing the seeds. Harvest time was in April or May. Fol-

lowing Hesiod's advice, farmers left their fields fallow for the rest of the spring and summer to enable the soil to replenish itself. The harvested grain was threshed, or separated from the stalks, by having mules trample it on a stone floor.

The planting calendar was different for other crops. Grapes, for example, were usually picked in September. Some of these were saved for eating but most were crushed by foot—as is still done in many places today—to make wine. Olives were harvested between October and January. Farmhands either picked the olives by hand or used

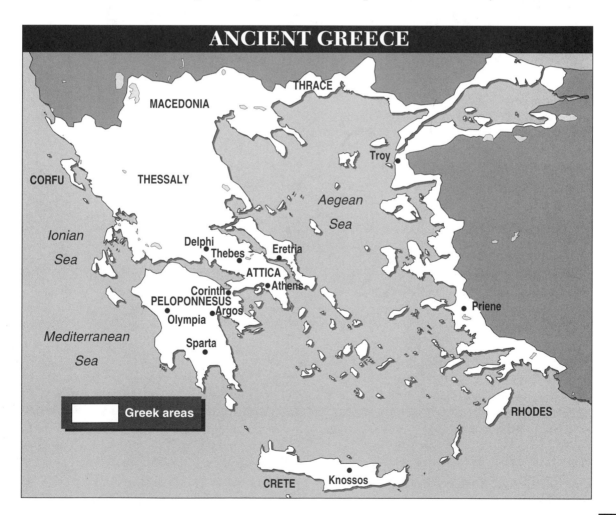

ANCIENT GREECE

THRACE

MACEDONIA

Troy

CORFU   THESSALY

Aegean
Sea

Ionian
Sea

Delphi
Thebes   Eretria
ATTICA
Corinth   ● Athens
PELOPONNESUS
Argos
Olympia   Priene

Mediterranean
Sea
Sparta

RHODES

Greek areas

CRETE   Knossos

Greek farmers harvest a crop, probably either wheat or barley, in the springtime. The oxen at left will pull the heavy sheaves to storage bins and later help transport the separated grain to market.

sticks to knock them out of the trees. The Greeks ate some of the olives and used the rest to make olive oil, which they used for cooking, making beauty products, and as fuel in oil lamps.

To supplement both their diets and their incomes, many farmers kept livestock, including cows, sheep, goats, and pigs. With few exceptions, only the larger, richer farms could afford to raise horses, which were expensive to feed and house. But rich farms were rare. In fact, except for the relatively few big landowners, most Greek farmers were poor and felt blessed when they managed to feed themselves and pay their debts. This was what prompted Herodotus's famous remark, "Poverty is always the foster-sister of Greece."[31] Indeed, a typical farmer, along with his wife, children, and the few servants and helpers he might be able to afford to pay

on a seasonal basis, worked from sunup to sundown for very few material rewards.

Yet most farmers found a different kind of reward in their country life. They considered being close to and working the land an ancient and time-honored lifestyle and farming the most honest of professions. Aristotle expressed that idea in his *Economics*, saying, "Agriculture should be ranked first [among professions] because it is just."[32] Farmers also felt that their fields, no matter how poor their yield, were their only cherished possession and proudly passed them on from one generation to another. The sixth-century B.C. writer Theognis of Megara captured part of this feeling in this lament of a farmer exiled from his polis: "It wounded my heart black that others own my flowering lands, and not for me are mules dragging the curved plow, now, in my exile, on the wretched sea."[33]

City Streets and Markets

Greece's hot, dry climate influenced life in the city as well as the countryside. Abundant sunlight provided excellent natural lighting as well as fresh air. Most public activities, including shopping, group worship, athletic events, and democratic assembly meetings, took place outside. Houses were almost always painted white to reflect the sun and keep interiors cooler.

The layout and arrangement of houses and other buildings within a town was usually not very orderly. This was because most poleis were very old. Many began as little more than a central acropolis to which farmers and villagers ran for protection in dangerous times. Then, little by little people built streets and houses that fanned outward in haphazard patterns from the acropoli. There were occasional exceptions. In the fifth century B.C., for instance, the Greek architect Hippodamus laid out the streets of Athens's

new port of Piraeus on a rectangular plan. And shortly after the end of the Classic Age, the Greek city of Priene, in what is now Turkey, was built on an orderly rectangular grid pattern. Yet in all Greek cities, even the planned ones, most streets were less than twelve feet wide, giving these urban centers a crowded, jumbled appearance. The streets, especially the side streets, were dirty, too. Public sanitation was rare or nonexistent, and people routinely threw their garbage, as well as their personal sewage, in containers called "chamber pots," right out into the streets, where it rotted in the sun.

By contrast, the markets and public squares were much more open. The principal marketplace in a Greek town was called the agora. In Athens, explain scholars Marjorie and C. H. B. Quennell:

This was the center of town, and it was more or less surrounded by colonnaded walks [column-lined walkways] with

The Daunting Task of Survival

No matter how splendid the public buildings and achievements of their individual poleis, most Greeks remained poor. And because a polis encompassed large agricultural areas beyond the central city, most of the poor were farmers. In his book A Social History of Greece and Rome, *classical historian Michael Grant explains:*

"Primarily, in the Greek world, [the poor] were an agricultural phenomenon. For that world was overwhelmingly agricultural. This is a point which is all too easy to forget, when *polis* is mistranslated as 'city-state.' The *polis* was not only the town, but the

country around it, in which the vast bulk of the population worked, in . . . villages and farms. . . . The vast majority of the population were peasants. . . . Mediterranean culture . . . depended . . . on seasonal labor, generally hired, and mainly free. Those who worked on the land . . . did not earn very much, and were always poor, and had little to eat. Their lives were precarious [uncertain]. . . . 'Freedom' [which so many Greeks enjoyed] did not help to guarantee a secure food supply. True, laborers on the land had a better chance to find food than a townsman . . . but all the same their task of sheer physical survival was daunting."

A drawing of an Athenian street. Most Greek city streets were narrow, cramped, and filthy.

shops behind. These would not have been much more than openings in the wall, with the counter in the opening. In the center of the agora were the stalls of the peasants [farmers] who brought in their vegetables and fowls and eggs for sale.[34]

The longest and most beautiful colonnaded building in the Athenian agora was the Painted Stoa, on the walls of which artists depicted various scenes. One entire wall was devoted to a magnificent painting, unfortunately now lost, showing the height of the Battle of Marathon, in which the Athenians defeated the Persians in 490 B.C.

A polis's agora typically had many other features. For example, metics and other craftspeople had shops located along its sides. They and merchants from other cities also utilized *kykloi*, platforms about four to six feet high on which they displayed goods ranging from pots and utensils to textiles and slaves. Public officials known as *agoranomoi* regularly policed the farm stalls and craft displays checking on the quality of the goods. If a person repeatedly tried to sell inferior merchandise, he received a fine. The agora also had a large altar for group worship and places where both men looking for work and employers who were hiring could meet and strike deals.

One feature of the agora that was particularly popular with Greek men was the barber shop. Most Greek men paid a great deal of attention to their hair and wanted to display the latest style. The barber shop had other allures as well. Robinson writes:

> Another operation performed at the barber's was treatment of the eyes for ophthalmia [redness and swelling], a complaint rendered very common by the dust of the streets. While awaiting his turn, [a customer] would chat with many others who were similarly engaged. The barber's shop was a recognized center for picking up gossip.[35]

Temple Architecture

For the most part, Greek houses and shops were rather simple and small, whereas public buildings tended to be large and imposing. For example, the Theater of Dionysus, nestled along the side of the Athenian Acropolis, had a huge *theatron*, a semicircular seating area comprised of rising stone tiers, that sat over fourteen thousand people. The circular, stone-lined orchestra, or performing area, was some eighty-five feet across.

Perhaps the most numerous, imposing, and beautiful of Greek public buildings were the religious temples. Each was dedicated to a certain god or goddess and often doubled as a storehouse for gold, jewels, and other treasures, public and private. Scholar Thomas Craven describes the form of a Greek temple:

A rectangle, with a low-pitched gable roof resting on side walls, and with columns to support a front porch [portico]—and sometimes a back porch—and a colonnade running down the sides. In its early stages, it was a limestone affair, with two, or four, wooden columns at the front to bear the weight of an extended roof. In its final development [in the Classic Age], it became a rectangular

marble structure with an encircling double row of columns, a portico at front and back, and a wide colonnade on either side. . . . The final product was composed entirely of marble, even to the translucent [partly transparent] tiles on the roof—and with sculptured embellishments [decorations] in the pediments [triangular gables] and the frieze [band of sculptures] running around the top of the walls under the colonnade.[36]

Greek temple architecture had three distinguishing styles, or orders, based on the specific details of the supporting columns. Columns of the most popular order, the Doric, had simple circular capitals, or tops. The capitals of Ionic columns featured more

The Theater of Dionysus in Athens as it may have appeared in the third and second centuries B.C., after generations of added structural features and ornamental decorations.

intricate, spiral- or scroll-shaped ornaments called volutes. The most elaborate order was the Corinthian, having capitals covered with carvings of sprouting, curving leaves.

Other kinds of decorations added to a temple's beauty. The sculptures, often life-size or larger, which stood in the triangular pediments and lined the side friezes, were magnificent works of art. Greek sculptors, such as the fifth-century B.C. master Phidias, had keen eyes and studied the nude male body in various settings, including gymnasiums and sporting events. They used paid or volunteer models to study the female form. The results were stunningly lifelike, even godlike, statues. As Craven puts it:

> From the mastery of movement and anatomy, the Athenian artists proceeded to ideal forms and faces . . . figures, male and female, beyond those produced by nature . . . marbles that reveal living flesh within the polished surfaces, faces of god-like serenity.[37]

These figures were coated with tinted waxes or paints; the frieze backgrounds and the pediments were painted bright colors, especially reds and blues.

The Culmination of Culture

The most famous of all Greek temples was the Parthenon, dedicated to Athena, goddess of war and wisdom and Athens's patron deity. This building and the other splendid edifices of the temple complex adorning Athens's Acropolis became much more than the focus of public religious ritual. The Acropolis was then, and remains today, the visual and cultural symbol not only of the Athenian polis, but of classical Greek cities in general. So

impressive were the Acropolis and Athena's temple that a later traveler to Athens was moved to remark, "All the world's culture culminated in Greece, all Greece in Athens, all Athens in its Acropolis, and all the Acropolis in the Parthenon."[38]

The first version of the Parthenon met destruction at the hands of the Persians when they captured the city in 480 B.C. during the Greek and Persian wars. In the 440s, Pericles undertook the building of a new Parthenon on a grander scale. As the most powerful and influential Athenian government leader for some thirty years, he helped to create the city's brief but brilliant "Golden Age" in the mid-to-late fifth century B.C. During this period, the government granted a generation of gifted artists, sculptors, builders, and craftspeople complete artistic freedom and almost unlimited funding. "It was not merely a passion for building," explains Greek scholar John Miliadis.

> It was not the political consideration that the construction of these great works would give work to the people for many years . . . nor was it merely an exhibition of power. It was something deeper than all this. It was the irrepressible need of a whole generation, which took the highest intellectual view of life, to find a creative self-expression.[39]

The creative aspect aside, the project *did* give thousands of Athenians and other Greeks full-time work for decades. The ancient historian Plutarch described these workers and vividly revealed the wide variety of trades and professions that existed in a large Greek city of the time:

> The materials to be used were stone, bronze, ivory, gold, ebony, and cypress-

The magnificent Parthenon featured eight columns in the front and seventeen along the side, in contrast to the ratio of six-to-thirteen that was customary in most other Greek temples.

wood, while the arts or trades which wrought or fashioned them were those of carpenter, modeler, coppersmith, stonemason, dyer, worker in gold and ivory, painter, embroiderer, and engraver, and besides these the carriers and suppliers of the materials, such as merchants, sailors, and pilots for the sea-borne traffic, and wagon-makers, trainers of draught animals [to pull the wagons], and drivers for everything that came by land. There were also rope-makers, weavers, leatherworkers, roadbuilders and miners. Each individual craft, like a general with an army under his separate command, had its own corps of unskilled laborers at its disposal.[40]

The workers' long labors produced spectacular results. A grand stone staircase led up the side of the hill to the Propylaea, a monu-

mental and magnificent colonnaded entranceway. Beyond this portal, on the summit of the Acropolis, stood three temples—the Erectheum, the Temple of Wingless Victory, and the Parthenon. Between and surrounding these were walkways of polished marble, dozens of towering statues, and numerous outdoor altars. Dominating the complex was the Parthenon, designed by the architect Ictinus and decorated by Phidias, an awesome structure 237 feet long, 110 feet wide, and 60 feet high. The sculptures in one of its pediments depicted the birth of Athena, while those in the other showed her rivalry with her uncle, the sea god Poseidon. Phidias's 525-foot-long frieze winding around the perimeter above the colonnade presented

a cross section of everyday Athenian life. In a magnificent procession representing . . . an annual festival in honor of the

A Vision of Life in a Perfect Building

The following two scholarly views of the famed Parthenon, one emphasizing the mechanics of its construction, the other the human spirit behind the work, are equally valid. The first is by art historian Thomas Craven in The Pocket Book of Greek Art, *and the second by Greek scholar John Miliadis in* The Acropolis.

"The Doric masterpiece [the Parthenon] was . . . proportioned inside and out, from floor to roof, with mathematical allowances for optical illusions. The height of the columns was five times their diameter to insure proper slenderness . . . and in every measurement of the building, the combined effect of harmony was taken into account. The floor, for example, was slightly rounded in the center to give the effect of a level surface when viewed from a short distance; the columns bulged a little in the middle . . .

and were tilted delicately towards the interior; and the metopes, or sculptured slabs between the triglyphs [ornamental squares], were actually oblongs, but when seen from the ground level appeared as squares. Behold the Parthenon, the only perfect building erected by man.

In a first glance at the Parthenon, we can appreciate the faultless work of the craftsman. . . . But though such craftsmanship is within our calculations [perceptions], what . . . forever enslaves [awes] us, is the feeling of life that springs up from the immortal work. To what is it due? What is it that distinguished the Parthenon from all other Doric temples, its brethren? The Parthenon is the severe Doric law inspired by the Attic [Athenian] feeling; it is clear reasoning, and yet filled with humanity; it is not directed to the mind so much as to the eye and the soul; it means to move the spirit and to ennoble it. It is more like a living organism than a mechanical creation. It is more the work of inspiration than of calculation. It is a new vision of life, the vision of classical Athenians."

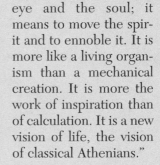

The ruins of the Parthenon as they appear today. Most of the damage occurred in 1687, when a cache of Turkish gunpowder stored inside the monument exploded.

A reconstruction of the interior main room, or cella, of the Parthenon as it may have looked in the late Classic Age. The giant statue of the goddess Athena was designed by the great sculptor Phidias.

goddess, horseman, magistrates, maidens . . . and exotic residents of the city move forward toward the majestic grouping of gods portrayed on the temple facade [pediments], benevolent but aloof from the world of mankind.[41]

Inside the Parthenon, in a large front chamber called the cella, was Phidias's dazzling statue of Athena, standing forty feet high and wrought of wood, ivory, and more than twenty-five hundred pounds of pure gold.

Civic Pride

In a sense, the Acropolis complex was for the Athenian city-dweller what the family farm was to the country farmer—the symbol of a way of life. The great public buildings exem-

Greek Public Buildings

The Greeks applied their considerable building talents mainly to huge and elaborate public buildings in their central cities. By contrast, their houses, both in the city and the countryside, were usually small, simple, and plain. In the Classic Age, temples and other large public buildings were constructed primarily of limestone and marble, although other materials, including wood and terra-cotta, a baked mixture of sand and clay, were also used.

To construct such buildings, workers used wagons to haul blocks of stone from quarries to the construction sites. After masons using hammers and chisels shaped the blocks on the ground, workers used ropes and pulleys to lift the pieces and wooden levers to position them in the structure. The columns consisted of several cylindrical pieces, the drums, which were stacked on top of one another and joined with metal pegs. Workers carved vertical grooves, or fluting, into most columns to give them an added graceful and detailed look.

Temples, with their pediments, colonnades, and pitched roofs, were the most common public buildings and nearly every polis had several, each dedicated to a certain god. Each polis also had a treasury, a smaller structure that physically resembled a temple, to store state monies. Theaters, open-air structures consisting of a circular stone orchestra, or acting area, and many rising rows of stone seats, were also common, as were stoas, colonnaded walkways with shops and offices behind them. Another popular kind of public building was the tholos, a round structure with a conical roof supported by a ring of columns. The most famous tholos was the one in Athens in which the Council of 500 met.

---

plified and highlighted the city as the center of government, culture, and social activities. City residents gazed upon the Acropolis with awe and great pride. And yet, the country folk could and did feel civic pride for the cultural achievements of their city brethren, for they too belonged to the clans, phratries, and tribes that made up the polis. A Greek polis was much like a wagon wheel with the farms and villages forming its spokes and rim and the city, with its acropolis, markets, and public buildings, forming its hub.

Pride in one's polis was perhaps greatest of all in Athens, where people of all walks of life seemed to sense that their city was special. Their pride stemmed partly from the realization that what they had built would outlast them, that the Acropolis, at least, would remain an object of awe and inspiration for future generations. The temples on that glorious summit, said Plutarch, "were created in so short a span, and yet for all time. . . . A bloom of freshness hovers over these works . . . and preserves them from the touch of time."[42] Indeed, today, even in ruin, these works have not lost their grandeur or allure. They remain a thrilling reminder of what a Greek city was and what it could achieve. Pericles himself said it best. "Future ages will wonder at us," he correctly predicted, "as the present age wonders at us now."[43]

Houses and Their Contents: How a Greek Home Operated

CHAPTER **3**

While the polis, in particular its acropolis and agora, was the center of Greek political and social life, the home was the focus of family life. As it is today, the home was the chief location of such activities as sleeping, cooking, dining, and grooming. Each household and the *oikos* that dwelled in it had its male head. He might answer to or take advice from more senior members of his clan or phratry, but concerning matters in his own home his word was law. His wife or mother, the "woman of the house," actually ran the household on a day-to-day basis and made many important decisions, but the fam-

A Greek country house, or villa. The bust on the pillar near the front door is a herm, *a representation of the god Hermes.*

ily head always had the last word. He distributed money to family members, hired servants or bought slaves, and arranged for his children's education. In a way, the Greek home, with its leader, various subordinate relatives and servants, chain of command, and expected roles and duties, was like a miniature version of the polis. Plato expressed this idea in his *Statesman*, writing, "A large household may be compared to a small state."[44]

How Houses Were Constructed

Greek homes were, with few exceptions, much more modest in size and in physical appearance than their modern counterparts. Most farmhouses, for instance, were little more than one- or two-room stone or log huts equipped with a crude hearth in the main room. Well-to-do country villas and many townhouses were larger and more functional. But even these were pitifully small and unadorned in comparison to the public buildings in an average polis. If no traces of the great temples and other magnificent state structures had survived, modern researchers might have concluded that ancient Greece was a primitive land. Classical scholar Ian Jenkins comments:

> The houses of Athens in the fifth century B.C. [were] modest, and their appearance belied the great age in which their inhabitants lived. In contrast to the splendor of the city's public buildings with their elegant porticoed facades and ornate sculptures, domestic dwellings were unpretentious [humble and unassuming] and not intended to draw the eye of the spectator.[45]

A typical Greek townhouse was built on a stone foundation over which layers of sun-dried mud bricks were stacked to make the walls. Although the bricks were sometimes reinforced with wooden timbers, the walls were not very strong or durable. The mud bricks began to crumble after a few years, which meant that conscientious homeowners had to undertake frequent upkeep and repairs. It also meant that burglars could easily tunnel through the walls, as happened from time to time in the average city. The floors of such houses varied in composition over the centuries. In much of the Archaic Age, Charles Gulick explains,

> the ground floor of the house was simply the original earth beaten hard or strewn with pebbles. Later, the floors were paved with flag-stones or with mosaic [small tiles]. Mats and rugs were essential, and in the Periclean age the importation of rare and expensive rugs from the East [Asia Minor and Persia] became common.[46]

House roofs were covered with baked pottery tiles and pitched at angles to allow rain to run off.

The most visible part of a house's exterior, the front wall, which faced the street, was extremely simple and plain. Only a narrow wooden door and perhaps one or two tiny windows broke the monotony of the whitewashed wall. The door was narrow so that opening it would not interrupt traffic on the equally narrow, cramped street. In fact, homeowners whose front doors opened outward sometimes had to pay a special tax. The only decoration in the front exterior was the *herm*, consisting of a short pedestal about three or four feet high bearing a bust of the god Hermes, which stood beside the door.

Hermes was both the messenger god and patron of travelers, and it was thought that his likeness kept evil from entering the house.

Rooms and Their Functions

The insides of Greek houses were also relatively simple in design and execution. The central feature was the courtyard, which was roofless and open to the elements to take advantage of the abundant natural lighting. The courtyards of most houses had small altars at which household members prayed, and some also had wells that provided a convenient water supply. Doors and corridors lining the courtyard led to various rooms. Larger houses also featured stairways leading to a second story.

The most visible room from the courtyard was the exedra, or outside sitting/lounging area. Though covered with a roof and surrounded by a small colonnade, the exedra had one or two sides open to the inner court. Because it was protected from direct sunlight, yet open to fresh air and light, it was a very comfortable and popular part of the house.

Two less comfortable but more practical rooms were the kitchen and the bath. The kitchen had an open hearth, which held the fire used for cooking, as well as tables for food preparation and bins for storage. The bath usually contained a tub, slightly smaller than modern versions, made of terra-cotta. The tub had a drain through which water flowed, via a recessed channel in the floor, to the outside. The bath was also equipped with a basin, resting on a small table, used for washing the hands and face. Daily bathing was a must for almost all Greeks, who were an especially clean people. They looked down upon many foreigners who rarely bathed, and it was common when discussing such people to recite with a touch of scorn the Greek adage, "They wash only three times in their life—at birth, when they marry, and at death."[47]

Most household baths did not contain showers. But the Greeks, with their special fondness for bathing, showered often in public bathhouses. In fact, explain archaeologists Peter James and Nick Thorpe:

The first real showers, with plumbed-in water, were invented by the ancient Greeks. After exerting themselves in the stadium, ancient Greek athletes would freshen up in the kind of shower depicted on an Athenian vase of the fourth century B.C. Two shower rooms are shown [on the vase]. . . . Piped-in water sprays down on the bathers through showerheads shaped like the faces of boars and lions. Near the top is a rack or pole over which the [bathers] have draped their garments and towels. The whole scene is amazingly contemporary: apart from the animal showerheads, it would not be out of place in a modern gym.[48]

Modern scholars suspect that some of the wealthier homes in a polis had the luxury of baths equipped with their own showers.

The home bath area was also the scene of much personal grooming, especially by the women of the house. After bathing, a woman rubbed perfumed oil, most often olive oil, into her skin to help keep it from drying out in the hot dry weather. She might also apply oil to her hair to make it shine, which was considered fashionable. Then she put on her makeup. "The women of Athens," Gulick remarks, "paler than other women because they lived so much indoors, used cosmetics, white lead and rouge, and touched up their eyebrows with a metallic stain imported from Egypt."[49] After applying her makeup, a woman placed her cosmetics back in her makeup case, a wooden, pottery, or metal container sometimes called a *pyx*.

The woman was not finished grooming, of course, until she looked herself over in her mirror. The Greeks used many kinds and styles of mirrors, usually of polished bronze, silver, or both. In the fifth century B.C. they invented the box mirror so that women could check and adjust their makeup when outside the home. "Precursor of the modern compact," write James and Thorpe, "it was made of two metallic disks that fitted together, fastened with a hinge; one inner surface was polished to form the mirror, all the other sides being engraved."[50]

This vase painting shows two Greek women sharing a small, hand-held mirror.

Furniture, Lighting, and Heating

While the exedra, kitchen, and bath were communal areas used by all family members, the bedrooms were more private. Bedrooms were small and ranged in number from one or two in the smallest townhouses to four or more in larger homes. Usually the master of the house and his wife occupied the largest bedroom, from which came the term "master bedroom." The children usually shared a bedroom, although the eldest male son might have his own room. Servants and slaves also shared a bedroom.

The bedrooms, along with other rooms in the house, featured various items of furniture, many of which would be familiar in a modern home. Most furniture was constructed of wood but a few pieces, mostly lamp stands and small tables, were made of bronze. Beds and couches consisted of a sim-

ple wooden frame strung with leather strips and covered with a thin mattress and pillows. Five by two-and-a-half feet seems to have been the standard size for couches. Tables were of various shapes and often very short so that they could be pushed under couches when not in use. The largest, most comfortable chair, the *thronos*, which had arms and a padded seat, was reserved for the master. A more common, armless chair, the *klismos*, with a wooden back and a seat of crosshatched leather strips, appeared in the fifth century B.C. People also sat on stools, some with folding legs for easy storage. The Greeks did not have modern-style bureaus with drawers and instead used wooden chests and wicker baskets to store clothes and linens. The most common type of decorative furnishing was the wall tapestry, a colorful textile often woven by the women of the house.

Among the furniture items were the devices that supplied the home with heat and light. The bronze lamp stands held oil lamps, which were supplemented at first by torches and later by candles set in a candelabra, or multiple-candle holder. According to Gulick:

In the classical period we hear of earthenware [pottery] and bronze lamps, small, shallow vessels containing olive oil, with one or more holes for wicks, and in the fifth century B.C., imported Etruscan [Italian] candelabra began to add both light and ornament to the room. Nevertheless reading at night was difficult, and "burning the midnight oil," as an expression describing an assiduous [diligent] student, may be traced back to this era.[51]

The Greeks had no concept of central heating and had to rely on the warmth generated from their hearths and from braziers, metal containers that burned charcoal. These were small and portable, making them easy to move from room to room. Yet, for the most part, on the coolest nights Greek homes were chilly and drafty and the warmest place was beneath one's blankets.

A terracotta bas-relief depicts a Greek woman placing a blanket or garment in a storage chest. Other household items, including a basket, mirror, and drinking cup, are shown above her.

Introducing Order into Chaos

Although ancient Greek houses apparently featured fewer pieces of furniture than modern ones, the rooms were hardly bare. In addition to wall tapestries and other decorations, many everyday belongings were hung on hooks, laid out on tables, or scattered about. In his *Oeconomicus*, an essay explaining how to manage a household, the fourth-century B.C. Greek writer Xenophon listed the main contents of a country house as: implements of sacrifice, women's clothes and ornaments for festivals, men's clothing for festivals and war, mattresses and coverlets for the women's quarters and also for the men's, women's and men's shoes, weapons, devices for spinning and for grinding corn, pots and other utensils for cooking, bathing utensils, troughs for washing clothes, and plates and other tableware. "A Greek house would probably have appeared untidy and disorganized, if judged by a modern Western standard," remarked scholar E. A. Gardner in A *Companion to Greek Studies*, "though doubtless a good housewife introduced order into the chaos."

This scene (painted on the undersurface of a bowl) shows a symposium, or dinner party. A flute player (right center) entertains the reclining guests, while a slave (left) tends to a large wine container.

Typical Foods and Meals

Perhaps the most specialized room in a Greek house was the *andron*. In a way it corresponded to a modern dining room, except that it was almost always reserved for the master's use. It was in the *andron* that he entertained his male guests at small banquet parties called symposiums. Occasionally, if he wanted to be a particularly big hit with his friends, he would hire one or more *hetairai* to entertain. But the most important feature of the *andron* and the parties staged in it was the food, which often took hours for the household women and servants to prepare.

On a more regular basis, of course, the women and servants had to prepare the family's daily meals. As a rule, the Greeks ate what people today would consider light meals. They did not care for red meat and only rarely, usually during religious festivals, ate mutton or pork. The more common meat items were fresh fish, rabbit, pigeon, and deer, which might be consumed a couple of times a week. The wealthy may have eaten these meats a bit more regularly. However, the bulk of most people's diets consisted of grains, fruits, and vegetables, usually eaten in moderate quantities. The famous adage coined by Plato's teacher, Socrates, "Bad men live to eat and drink, good men eat and drink to live," more or less captured the Greek attitude toward food.[52]

The first meal of the day was light indeed. Breakfast was usually nothing more than a piece of bread dipped and soaked in wine. Lunch consisted of bread, supplemented by cheese, olives, figs, dates, grapes, or currants. The latter, small raisins still eaten today, were at the time called "Corinths" after the polis in which they originated, but over the centuries the term gradually evolved into "currants."

Supper, taken most commonly in the late afternoon, was more substantial and varied. People of all classes favored a thick porridge made from barley, and most suppers featured this staple dish. This meal also included vegetables, of which the most common were beans, lentils, peas, garlic, lettuce, parsley, onions, mushrooms, artichokes, beets, and cucumbers. Thyme, coriander, and sesame were popular seasonings, and honey was used as a sweetener.

Apparently people liked their suppers piping hot, which, because they ate with their hands, sometimes burned the fingers. One common way of avoiding this was to hold a piece of hot food in a folded piece of bread. But some diners resorted to more extreme methods. James and Thorpe describe one diner:

Perfumes, Tweezers, and Egg Whites

Bathing was only the beginning of a Greek woman's daily round of personal grooming. Describing such grooming practices in his work The Life of Greece, *the renowned historian Will Durant wrote:*

"The [Greek] women also shave here and there, using razors or depilatories [hair removers] of arsenic and lime. Perfumes—made from flowers, with a base of oil—are numbered in the hundreds; Socrates complains that men [also] make so much use of them. Every lady of class has an armory of mirrors, pins, hairpins, safety pins, tweezers, combs, scent bottles, and pots for rouge and creams. Cheeks and lips are painted with sticks of minium or alkanet root . . . eyelashes are darkened, and then set with a mixture of egg white and gum ammoniac. Creams and washes are used for removing wrinkles, freckles, and spots."

One ingenious gourmet named Philoxenus spent hours hardening his fingers and gargling with near-boiling water so that he could pick up and swallow the hottest tidbit. Having developed these techniques, he was accused of bribing cooks to serve the dishes extra hot when he dined out so that he could gobble them up before the other guests could even taste them.[53]

By contrast, the Greeks liked their drinks chilled. Storing containers of liquid underground sometimes produced the desired effect. But those who could afford it used ice, which mule trains daily hauled into the city from the nearest mountains. The most popular drink was wine, which people diluted with water in a ratio of two parts water to one part wine. Writes C. E. Robinson:

The mixing was done by the [household] slaves in a large earthenware bowl. From this the drink was ladled into the cups—broad shallow saucers raised on a delicate base, often of exquisite design and [covered] with beautiful painted pictures.[54]

Suppers served at a symposium in the *andron* were more elaborate than the regular daily meals. The women and servants prepared special dishes; for example, an omelette composed of eggs, flour, cheese, honey, and sheep's brains served in a fig leaf. There were also special desserts such as cakes and various mixtures of olives, figs, and nuts. Male servants brought in the food, attended to the guests, and cleaned up. These duties were never performed by the household women because it was considered unseemly for them to mix in any way with the male guests.

The Efficient, Harmonious Home

Women's exclusion from men's gatherings was just a part of the collection of traditional limitations and duties imposed upon females by a male-dominated society. In fact, when not involved somehow in the kitchen or bath, the women of the house spent most of their hours secluded in the *gynaeceum* (or *gynaikonitis*), the "women's quarters." This area consisted of one or more large utility rooms in which women engaged in spinning, weaving, and visiting with female friends. The Roman writer Cornelius Nepos, who visited Greece not long after the Classic Age, found such segregation of women odd and compared it unfavorably to the custom in his own land:

> Much that we hold to be correct in Rome is thought shocking in Greece. No Roman thinks it an embarrassment to take his wife to a dinner party. At home the wife holds first place, and is the center of its social life. Things are very different in Greece, where the wife is never

Greek women and children, attended by household slaves, lounge in the gynaeceum, *the "women's quarters," of a well-to-do home.*

The Last Word in Elegance

Another part of a Greek woman's beauty regimen was choosing and applying jewelry that matched the particular makeup and outfit she was wearing that day. This excerpt from scholar Thomas Craven's The Pocket Book of Greek Art *explains what such jewelry looked like and how we know about it.*

"An infallible sense of fitness, of proportioning, of the ultimate and only way to use materials to be transformed into objects of art, is attested to by Greek jewelry. . . . [It] is the last word in elegance and craft—not made to dazzle the eye, but with inexpressible delicacy in weaving gold threads into neckbands and attaching filigree [lacelike] ornaments in the shape of hanging beads or globules [spheres]. Surfaces were decorated with natural forms of plants and animals, or tiny mythological figures such as winged victories and cupids; and the pendant attachments to earrings and bracelets were relieved [decorated] by the minute heads of lions and rams, exquisitely modeled but without the . . . [modern] Hollywood artiness [gaudiness]. These priceless examples of Greek art have been largely preserved in tombs, and along with gems and coins, are virtually the only productions of pure Greek genius that have come down to us as they were originally made."

These ornate earrings are typical of the fine gold, silver, and bronze jewelry items many Greek women owned and wore.

present at dinner, unless it is a family party, and spends all her time in a remote part of the house called the Women's Quarter, which is never entered by a man unless he is a very close relative.[55]

The reported speech of a father to a jury in a civil court case reveals how completely young women were segregated from men in the home. The man sought to impress the jury with the respectability of his family by bragging that his sister and nieces were "so well brought up that they [were] embarrassed in the presence even of a man who is a member of the family."[56]

Like other members of the household, women had their regular duties. In addition to spinning, weaving, and helping prepare meals, these included overseeing the female, and sometimes the male, servants, keeping the house clean and well organized, and supervising the children. The Greek writer

Xenophon, who, like most Greek men, believed in keeping women "in their place," was more specific. He lectured to women:

Your business will be to stay indoors and help to dispatch the servants who work outside, while supervising those who work indoors. You will receive incoming revenue [from the master] and pay the necessary [household] expenses with it. . . . When wool is delivered to you, you will see that garments are made for those that need them, and take care that the dried grain is kept ready for eating. And there is another of your duties which I'm afraid may seem to you rather thankless—you will have to see that any of the servants who is ill gets proper treatment.[57]

The servants the woman of the house managed, a mix of slaves and freedmen, had their own duties. Besides helping with the cooking, serving meals, and doing much of the cleaning, they did most of the shopping, washed the family clothes by hand, and performed all difficult manual labor. Those who put in long years of service were regarded as members of the family, treated decently, and often paid small but regular wages. Some servants were so efficient and trustworthy that their masters gave them more important responsibilities. A few of these domestics, in the absence of the master's wife or mother, actually ran the entire household. It is hardly surprising, then, that many servants were outspoken and freely offered their opinions

Greek servant women converse while filling jugs with water at a communal fountain.

or advice, which the master often accepted. Such relationships were common enough to prompt Plato to exclaim, "My domestics became on some occasions my masters."[58]

The head of the Greek household may have been the boss, but the wise man realized that without the contributions of women and servants his home could not run efficiently. As is still true today, the most harmonious and loving homes were those in which everyone was treated fairly and with respect.

Social Customs and Entertainment: The Pursuit of Leisure

The Greeks had distinct social customs, habits, and traditions that set them apart from other ancient peoples. These included clothing and hairstyles, attitudes toward love and courting, marriage and divorce practices, group interactions and games, and the pursuit of leisure activities. Greek social life was diverse and rich and based on personal communication and interaction. By contrast, much of modern social life depends on electronic media and nonpersonal communication. Instead of telephones, fax machines, radio, television, and movies, the Greeks enjoyed meeting at daily community events, gossip sessions, private parties, and banquets; marriage celebrations lasting days and involving hundreds of people; poetry and music recitations, both private and public; public meetings, discussion groups, and clubs; religious festivals and banquets; athletic games and competitions of all sorts; and all-day theatrical performances. This speech from Aristophanes' *Peace* suggests that simple, diverse social pastimes and interactions could keep a Greek happy:

Then will be the time for laughing,
Shouting out in jovial glee,
Sailing, sleeping, feasting, chugging wine,
All the public sights to see.
Then the cottabos [parlor game] be
    playing,
Then be hip-hip-hip-hurrahing,

Pass the day and pass the night
Like a regular Sybarite [resident of
    Sybaris, a city known for its social life
    and physical pleasures].[59]

Clothes and Hairstyles

Some of the most visually obvious and important social customs involved clothing and hairstyles. The Greeks were extremely conscious of their physical appearance; being dirty, slovenly, or unkempt was socially unacceptable under all conditions. They wanted to look their best for every occasion, even for such mundane activities as walking through the streets or visiting friends. So, both men and women made sure that their clothes and hairstyles were always neat, attractive, and fashionable.

Most Greek clothes were beautiful to look at but rather simple in design and shape. Ian Jenkins explains the style:

To a large extent the rectangular shape of the loom determined the shape of the clothes people wore. Today we are used to large factory-produced rolls of material, cut up into convenient shapes tailored to fit the body. The ancient loom, however, produced relatively short, rectangular pieces of cloth, which could be draped directly onto the body without the need

Greek buildings were graceful and ornate in appearance. Likewise, many Greek garments were elegant and fashionable.

for cutting into shape. . . . Thus there was no wastage and, in an age before the sewing machine, stitching was kept to a minimum. Pins, tucks and belts were used to keep the garment in place and, if necessary, to adjust the length.[60]

The most common garment, worn by both men and women, was the chiton, or basic tunic, which consisted of a single rectangular piece of cloth. Women generally wore the chiton ankle length and fastened it at the top with buttons, pins, or brooches. "A girdle [belt] of gold, silver or linen handsomely embroidered," writes Gulick, "gave variety of lines, according to whether it was

placed just below the breast, or allowed to hang more loosely round the hips."[61] Men's chitons were usually sewn up at the sides and worn about knee length, although ankle length was common for old men and on very formal occasions. The himation was another, but larger, rectangular piece draped around the body. A woman's himation might be a loose traveling cloak that covered her from head to foot, while a man usually wound his himation tightly around his body and threw the end over one shoulder.

Among the many clothing accessories were large, light-weight, and often brightly colored scarves or shawls that women draped over their chitons or himations. Men, especially younger men and soldiers, sometimes wore an outer cloak called a *chlamys*, which they fastened at one shoulder with a brooch or pin. Because of the warm climate, many Greeks went barefoot much of the time, especially in the home. However, shoes and boots were not uncommon and were usually made of leather with long straps that could be tied in different ways to alter the style. The climate also dictated the frequent wearing of hats for protection from the sun. One of the most common hats was the Thessalian *petasos*, which had a low crown, wide brim,

and a cord on which the hat hung along the upper back when the wearer flipped it off.

Greek men and women were as particular about their hair as they were about their clothes and kept their hair clean and neatly trimmed. Hair and beard styles were fairly basic and changed only slowly. In the Archaic Age, all men wore their hair long, usually shoulder length, donned colorful headbands, and sported long beards throughout adult life. In the Classic Age following the Persian wars, shorter hair and beards became fashionable. A grown man without a beard was

The sculpture at left depicts a Greek woman wearing a long himation wrapped with the end thrown forward over the shoulder. The vase at right shows men clad in himations wrapped in varied styles.

still an extremely rare sight and the clean-shaven look did not come in until the late fourth century B.C. Regarding women's hair, Peach and Millard write, "Women always wore their hair long. In the Archaic [Age] it was held in place by a head band. In the Classic [Age] hair was usually worn up, held in place by ribbons, diadems, nets, or scarves."[62]

Love and Marriage

Certainly one of the most important reasons for neat, fashionable clothes and hairstyles was to appear attractive to the opposite sex. Although the seclusion of women in many poleis generally kept young unmarried men and women from mixing socially, they did see each other at religious festivals, clan and phratry functions, and the theater. On such occasions, a young person might meet and converse for the first time with his or her future spouse.

It would seem logical that, in a society in which men dominated and accorded women an inferior status, people married for reasons other than love. And to some extent this was certainly the case. Some men looked at a prospective wife more as an acquisition necessary for bearing children and keeping the house than as a soul mate. This fairly common attitude was expressed by a character shopping for a wife in a fourth-century B.C. comedic play: "A woman is a pest—that can't be helped. The luckiest man's the one who gets the least unbearable pest."[63]

Indeed, most of the social customs surrounding marriage did not encourage or even take into consideration the idea of falling in love. Most marriages were arranged, usually by clan or phratry heads, and some young couples hardly knew each other before their wedding nights. Money was a frequent con-sideration in planning marriage. A prospective bride's father provided her with a dowry, money and various valuables, which her husband acquired on marrying her. So it was not unusual for a man heavily in debt to see marriage to a woman with a handsome dowry as a partial solution to his money troubles. At the same time, some women were willing to marry men they detested in order to acquire prestige, a fine home, and lifelong security. Theognis criticized such matches:

> The noblest man will marry the lowest daughter of a base family, if only she brings in money. And a lady will share her bed with a foul rich man, preferring gold to pedigree [family reputation]. Money is all [that is important].[64]

Even worse, some young women were forced by law to marry a specific person. Athenian girls without brothers, known as *epikleroi*, had to wed the nearest relative on their father's side, beginning with his brother.

Yet despite all these impediments to genuine affection, some Greek men and women did love each other, often passionately. Descriptions of flaming young love are fairly common in Greek plays, as in this exchange from comic playwright Menander's *The Grouch*:

> CHAEREAS: What was it you said, Sostratos? You saw a girl, a free-born girl here . . . and you fell in love at once?
>
> SOSTRATOS: At once.
>
> CHAEREAS: Fast work. Surely you'd made your mind up, when you first set out from home, to fall in love with someone?
>
> SOSTRATOS: You laugh, Chaereas; but I'm in a bad way [aching with love].[65]

A powerful force behind the ancient Greeks' rich array of social activities was their leisure ethic, or set of concepts and values regarding leisure time: who should have it and how it should be spent. In their book Ancient Inventions, *scholars Peter James and Nick Thorpe comment:*

"The Greeks of classical times were the first to have a developed leisure ethic. Ancient Greek civilization reached its zenith during the fifth and fourth centuries B.C. when the ruling classes (about 20 percent of the overall population) were entirely freed from work by the extensive use of slaves and serfs. . . . Since their only duties were occasional political and military ones, the citizens . . . had a considerable amount of free time on their hands. Many of course sat around . . . engaging in philosophical discourse, including discussion of which activities were suitable as leisure for the rest of the population. Cerebral activities such as music and theater . . . were favored. . . . For those who preferred more active pursuits, there were parks and gymnasia for exercise and a wide variety of sports. Modern Westerners would find themselves comfortably entertained if they could somehow be transported back to Athens in the fourth century B.C.—given of course that they were in the upper classes."

From Wedding to Divorce

Whatever the reasons for marrying, the Greek wedding was always both a solemn and festive occasion. Shortly before the ceremony, the bride collected her childhood toys and sacrificed them to Artemis, the virgin goddess who was thought to protect young girls and pregnant women. In Athens and most poleis, on the wedding day the bride's and groom's families prayed to the gods and feasted separately in their own homes. In early evening, the groom, accompanied by his *parochos*, or best man, traveled to the bride's house. The bride and groom climbed into a horse-drawn chariot—in poorer families a simple cart—and rode to the groom's house, accompanied by a procession that included wedding guests, torch bearers, dancers, and musicians. There, according to Jenkins:

The newly-weds were met by the groom's mother, who came out bearing torches to light their way across the threshold. The groom led his bride through the door towards the family hearth. At the place that represented the nucleus of the bride's future domestic life, the bride and groom knelt down and bowed their heads under a shower of nuts and sweetmeats (*katakysmata*), tokens of the prosperity it was hoped their union would bring to the house.[66]

With all of the guests crowded about, a solemn ceremony, about which little is known, took place at the hearth. The following day, a huge party, which included the presentation of wedding gifts and a banquet, took place at the groom's house.

The exception to this form of wedding ceremony was in Sparta, where marriage, like nearly all other social customs, was influenced by the harsh military *agoge*. Plutarch left behind this chilling description of a Spartan wedding night:

Wedding guests celebrate the marriage of a young couple at a reception held outside a fashionable Greek home.

For their marriages the women were carried off by force. . . . After the woman was thus carried off, the bride's maid, so called . . . cut her hair off close to the head, put a man's cloak and sandals on her, and laid her down on a pallet, on the floor, alone in the dark. Then the groom . . . after supping at his mess-table as usual, slipped stealthily into the room where the bride lay . . . and bore her in his arms to the marriage bed. Then, after spending a short time with his bride, he went away composedly to his usual quarters, there to sleep with the other young men.[67]

Though not a common occurence, some Greek marriages were not successful and

ended in divorce. Not surprisingly, divorce customs were weighted heavily in favor of men. A man who wanted a divorce simply made a formal declaration of his intent in front of witnesses. He almost always kept custody of the children and sent his former wife to live with one of her male relatives. A woman could divorce her husband but because women were not allowed to bring cases into court she had to appeal to one of the city archons. After examining her written statement, he might grant her the divorce and in very rare cases allow her to keep the children. The chief grounds for both men's and women's divorces was *moikheia*, or adultery. Only rarely was a male adulterer prosecuted by his wife's father or brothers, but when he was the penalty could be severe. If caught in the act, he could be imprisoned until he paid a heavy fine, or even killed.

Parties, Games, Discussions, and Gossip

Perhaps one reason why so many Greek marriages, even loveless ones, stayed intact was that most husbands and wives were just too busy or distracted to get involved in complicated domestic disputes. A majority of Greeks, certainly those in Athens and the more cultured poleis, were almost constantly involved in one aspect or another of the rich social life that included various clan and phratry functions, religious festivals, and weddings and other large social functions that lasted for days and were accompanied by feasts.

Even more frequent, of course, were the symposiums held in individual homes. Dozens, or even hundreds, of such dinner parties, each with probably four to fifteen guests, might be held on any given night in a large polis. In addition to food and conversation, the symposiums often featured drinking songs, accompanied by the lyre, or harp. One favorite pastime was for each guest, in turn, to make up a verse, always connected somehow in theme to the preceding one. One surviving drinking song goes:

At this symposium held in the andron *of a Greek townhouse, the guests eat and converse while male servants see to their needs.*

Fruitful earth drinks up the rain;
Trees from earth drink that again;
Sea drinks air, and soon the sun
Drinks the sea and him the moon.
Is it reason then, do you think,
I should thirst when all else drink?[68]

To enliven their symposiums even more, hosts sometimes hired musicians, dancers, and acrobats to perform.

Another persistent feature of symposiums, and of Greek leisure life in general, was the playing of games. As classical scholar Edith Hamilton puts it, "The Greeks were the first people in the world to play and they played on a great scale. All over Greece there were games, all sorts of games."[69] Perhaps the most popular party game was *cottabos*, described by James and Thorpe as a

rather silly and extremely messy game to go with wine drinking. . . . According to tradition, this was invented by a light-headed Greek . . . [who], during the course of some heavy drinking, bet his friends that he could hit the lamp on the top of its stand with the dregs in the bottom of his cup. This new form of entertainment . . . was cashed in on by a crafty merchant, who invented special cottabos stands. Precariously balanced on the top of each stand was a bronze disk. The idea of the game was to knock this off with the wine dregs so that it fell onto a lower metal disk, which then rang like a bell.[70]

Another popular game, the invention of which Herodotus credited to the Lydians of Asia Minor, was knucklebones, played by both men and women. A person threw five small animal bones into the air one at a time and tried to catch them on the back of his or her hand.

Love and Self-Sacrifice

Although women were generally viewed as men's inferiors and loveless marriages were common, some Greek men recognized that women were in many ways their equals and allowed themselves to fall deeply in love with their wives. Ancient playwrights portrayed variations of this theme. An excellent example was Euripides' tragedy Alcestis *(here quoted from* The Norton Book of Classical Literature*), in which the author showed how the title character, a woman, was capable of the same qualities of loyalty, love, courage, and self-sacrifice normally attributed to men. In the play, Admetos, king of Thessaly, who had been fated to die young, receives a boon from the gods. He can live a long life, but only if he can manage to find someone who is willing to die in his place. He finds that only his wife, Alcestis, possesses the necessary courage and depth of love, both of which she demonstrates by giving her life. At the funeral, Admetos's father, Pheres, delivers these lines:*

"Son, I have come to help you bear the burden of your grief. You have lost a good wife: a decent, loving, humble wife. A hard and bitter loss, but bear it you must. . . . We must honor her in death as she deserves; she gave her life to let you keep the light. . . . And by her bravery in death, she has been a credit—no, a glory—to her sex. . . . Mark my words, son. Marriage is for most of us a losing proposition. But this wife of yours was pure gold."

People buy and sell, converse, strike deals, mill about, and relax in the wide-open agora of a Greek city. The city's acropolis can be seen in the distance.

Banquets, parties, and games made up just one aspect of Greek social life and entertainment. Public meetings, such as those of Athens's Assembly, Council, and law courts, were numerous. Leisure moments that preceded and followed the official portions of these meetings afforded citizens, mainly men, the opportunity to mill about, converse, and exchange gossip and ideas. Likewise, the agora and other markets and public squares were common places for groups of people to meet and discuss politics, philosophy, and all manner of more trivial topics. Gymnasiums were also social gathering spots. In addition to physical exercise, these facilities often featured small libraries and daily lectures on diverse subjects. It was not uncommon for young men to linger in a gym for hours, intently discussing the contents of a lecture heard earlier. Young men's clubs, with catchy names such as "the Independents" and "the Rips," were popular, too.

Greek Theater

Perhaps the most formal and elaborate social gathering outside of the largest religious festivals was the theater. A unique combination of art form and public entertainment, the theater originated in Athens in the sixth century B.C. Its subsequent development was rapid and spectacular. In less than a century, theater evolved from a series of informal songs and speeches recited by worshipers in roadside religious processions to formal plays performed by troupes of actors in magnificent public facilities. Almost all of the theatrical concepts familiar today, including tragedy, comedy, slapstick, acting, directing, costumes, scenery, and even acting awards and theater tickets, developed in Greece in the early Classic Age.

In Athens, theater was part of the City Dionysia, a lavish yearly festival that honored Dionysus, god of fertility, who, people

The Greek Chorus

Most Greek tragedies employed a special stage convention called the chorus, which consisted of a group of actors who usually spoke in unison, sang, and danced. The chorus served several functions in a play. It interacted with the actors, giving advice, asking questions, and expressing opinions, thereby helping the audience interpret and understand the plot and themes. Through its movements and vocal tone, which might be happy or sad, the chorus also set the play's overall mood. An excellent example of the chorus's performing all these functions appears in Aeschylus's The Persians *(quoted here from* The Complete Greek Drama*). After being defeated by the Greeks, Persian king Xerxes is in a state of despair.*

CHORUS
O Wo, Wo, Wo! Unspeakable wo
The demons of revenge have spread. . . .
XERXES
Dismay, and rout [defeat], and ruin, ills that wait

On man's afflicted fortune, sink us down.
CHORUS
Dismay, and rout, and ruin on us wait,
And all the vengeful storms of Fate:
Ill flows on ill, on sorrows sorrows rise. . . .
Is all your glory lost?
XERXES
See you these poor remains of my torn robes?
CHORUS
I see, I see. . . . I thought these Greeks shrunk appalled
At arms [were afraid to fight].
XERXES
No: they are bold and daring: these sad eyes
Beheld their violent and dreadful deeds.
CHORUS
The ruin, you say, of your shattered fleet?
XERXES
And in the anguish of my soul I tore
My royal robes.
CHORUS
Wo, wo!

believed, oversaw the annual cycle of the seasons. As the festival opened in late March, a splendid procession of thousands of people wound its way through Attica, the streets of Athens, and into the Theater of Dionysus. There, for several days, playwrights presented their works.

At first tragedy was the most important and recognized dramatic form. The Greeks were the first people in the world to recognize clearly a great contradiction of human affairs, namely that ugliness inevitably coexists with beauty. In order to appreciate and embrace the good, they realized, one must accept, confront, and deal with the bad. As scholar Paul Roche explains:

The theme of all tragedy is the sadness of human life and the universality of evil. The inference the Greeks drew from this was *not* that life was not worth living, but that because it was worth living the obstacles to it were worth overcoming. Tragedy is the story of our existence trying to rear its head above the general shambles [life's darker elements].[71]

It was the eternal struggle to find beauty in ugliness and light in darkness that Greek tragedians explored in their plays. "In tragedy," Hamilton remarks, "the Greek genius penetrated farthest and it is the revelation of what is most profound in them."[72]

The three recognized masters of Greek tragedy were Aeschylus, Sophocles, and Euripides, all of whom lived and wrote in fifth-century B.C. Athens.

In time, however, comedy became nearly as important to theatergoers as tragedy. Comedic playwrights, including the fifth-century master Aristophanes, often poked fun at political leaders and other well-known personalities in biting and hilarious satires of daily life. Greek comedy, theatrical historian James Butler writes, "contained an incredible mixture of high [intellectual] and low [indecent] comedy, satire, buffoonery, slapstick, verbal play . . . abuse, sex . . . singing, dancing, nudity, and vulgarity often in its crudest form."[73]

Audiences reacted to these comic displays loudly and enthusiastically, often applauding characters they liked and booing and hissing others. In contrast, during the tragedies audience behavior was more reserved, befitting the serious subject matter. Because a cycle of plays lasted most of the day and seating was of wood or stone, the spectators sat on cushions for comfort. They either brought the cushions with them or rented them from vendors, who also hawked fast food of all kinds prepared in portable kitchens set up outside the theater.

The theater, as well as many other social activities and services, was supported by a liturgy, or system of public contributions. Although metics paid direct taxes to the state, citizens in Athens and many other poleis did not. Therefore, the government called upon those who could afford it to pay for theatrical productions, the erection of statues and monuments, the distribution of foods for religious festivals, and other public services. Each year the names of new contributors to the liturgy were selected, in rotation, from lists of the more well-to-do citizens.

Most contributors took pride in this duty, and many tried to gain fame and prestige by outspending their colleagues. For example, a session of the yearly City Dionysia consisted of about eighteen dramatic presentations, each of which had a *choregus*, or wealthy backer. A typical expenditure by such a backer in the fifth century B.C. was between

This drawing re-creates a scene from a Greek theatrical comedy of the Classic Age. Note the use of elaborate masks to represent general character types, in this case an "old man" and a "mischievous slave."

Social Customs and Entertainment: The Pursuit of Leisure **57**

Poking Fun at Life

Aristophanes (ca. 445–ca. 388 B.C.) was one of the most brilliant and best-liked playwrights of his day. He wrote more than forty comedies, of which eleven have survived. Perhaps the most famous of these are Clouds, *which pokes fun at the philosopher Socrates and other intellectuals;* Birds, *in which Athens is compared to a city constructed in the sky by birds;* Lysistrata, *about Athenian women trying to stop a war by banding together in a sex strike against their husbands; and* Frogs, *a literary satire featuring Aristophanes' fellow dramatists, Aeschylus, Sophocles, and Euripides, as characters. One of Aristophanes' funniest plays is* Clouds, *in which, as scholar Robert B. Downs explains in* Books That Changed the World:

"An old man, overwhelmed by debt incurred by his horse-racing son . . . and pursued by creditors, hears that the great philosopher Socrates can teach his stu-dents to talk their way out of any predicament. . . . The father [Strepsiades] visits the 'Thinking Factory' of Socrates. There the master is found swinging above the ground in a basket in order to observe more closely the secrets of the universe. . . . His disciples are seen in strange, undignified positions, bent over scanning the sand."

Strepsiades approaches another student, and the following exchange (quoted from *The Complete Plays of Aristophanes*) ensues:

STREPSIADES: What manner of beasts are these? Why are their eyes riveted to the ground?
STUDENT: They are investigating what's under it.
STREPSIADES: Then why does [that fellow's] rump gaze heavenward?
STUDENT: His secondary interest is astronomy.

---

three hundred and fifteen hundred drachmas. But some *choregi* spent as much as three thousand or more drachmas in an age when four hundred drachmas was enough to support an average small family for a year. One late fifth century B.C. Athenian *choregus* bragged publicly that in one year:

> I spent three thousand drachmas, and another twelve hundred two months later when I won the prize with the men's chorus at the festival of the Thargelia . . . and at the [City] Dionysia I was victor with a men's chorus which cost me 1,500 drachmas. . . . Then I was choregus for a boys' chorus that cost me 1,500 drachmas.[74]

Thus, a large part of Greece's abundant social life and entertainments, from small private symposiums to vast celebrations and theater gatherings, was privately subsidized. The result was that wealth, though concentrated in the hands of a few individuals, frequently benefited all of society.

Business and Commerce: How Goods Were Made, Shipped, and Sold

Despite the Greeks' leisure ethic, abundant free time, and wide array of social and cultural activities, the majority of people worked on a full- or part-time basis. Most women were occupied at home with their household duties. Most farmers were too poor to leave their land and chores very often or for very long; their social life was probably limited to a handful of yearly religious festivals and clan get-togethers. Similarly, metics and slaves worked full-time and probably participated in very few social activities.

Even some of the better-off male citizens who could easily have taken advantage of a leisure system designed in their favor chose to work instead. "Many Athenians of the richer sort," comments Charles Gulick, "who could well afford to sit on juries without pay, renounced the 'leisure' which was the ideal of the philosopher and statesman, and were active in wholesale trade."[75] This belies the popular and idyllic notion that most Greeks spent their days playing sports and strolling through the streets engaged in philosophical discussion. In fact, those that took full advantage of the leisure system represented only a tiny portion of the population, perhaps 10 percent at most. The rest were involved in daily labor or business of one sort or another.

In the Archaic Age land ownership was the principal basis of wealth, and agriculture was the foundation of the economies of poleis. Yet commerce, which included local industries, retail selling, and trade, both foreign and among poleis, was a permanent and important fixture of the overall Greek economy. For one thing, not everyone could be or wanted to be a farmer. In addition, because of Greece's low rainfall and poor soil, farmers could not provide all of the food people needed and wanted. That meant importing some food, which inevitably involved shipping, merchants, markets, and trade. The Greeks also needed and desired other imported goods, such as Egyptian papyrus to write on and Persian rugs. In exchange for these and other commodities, the Greeks exported their own goods. Outgoing ships, Gulick writes, carried "cargoes of rich and varied earthenware and metal vessels, arms and armor, bronze statues and other works of art, furniture . . . olives, figs, and fish."[76] The buying, selling, and transport of these goods employed many Greeks—metics, slaves, and citizens alike—on a full-time basis.

The Growth of Commerce

Although the Greek economy remained agriculturally based in the Classic Age, the sixth and fifth centuries B.C. saw a sharp rise in the economic importance of commerce. This was partly due to the effects of widespread colonization. Athens, Corinth, Miletus, and many other Aegean poleis maintained political ties

Merchants hawk their wares and strike deals, while farmers sell fruits and vegetables at the Athenian agora.

and trade relations with their colonies all along the coasts of the Mediterranean and Black Seas. Pierre Léveque explains:

> The more prosperous of the new colonies soon spawned further colonial settlements of their own, thereby increasing their chances of continued success. Prosperity came quickly to the new Mediterranean colonies. In no time they were building whole complexes of temples equally as large and splendid as those of [their mother cities]. . . . It is no exaggeration to speak of Greece's western colonies [those in Italy, southern France, and Spain] as a new world, a prosperous culture whose citizens lived comfortably, traveled, and freely indulged in the pleasures of life.[77]

Each colony represented a valuable trading partner, not only for its mother city but also for other Greek or non-Greek cities in the Mediterranean sphere. Combining the Greek colonies with those founded by the Phoenicians, a Middle Eastern people known for their maritime commerce, the Mediterranean sphere supported more than 250 thriving trading centers by the late sixth century B.C.

Another factor that stimulated commerce, trade, and business activities was the rise of the Athenian empire in the fifth century B.C. Athens and Sparta led the successful defense of Greece against the invading Persians between 490 and 479 B.C. Athens, more populous, culturally advanced, and democratic than Sparta, emerged from the fray as the seeming champion of all Greeks. The city formed an Athenian-led federation of many Aegean and Mediterranean poleis with the intention of promoting self-protection and prosperity. Unfortunately, Athens quickly became a bully, imposed its own ideas on its allies, and turned the federation into its own empire. Yet that empire's vast trading network did bring increased prosperity to its members. Business and commerce, including shipping, local industries, and retail trade, expanded throughout the eastern Mediterranean. According to historian W. G. Hardy:

The Aegean was an Athenian lake. Athenian warships guarded the entrance to the Black Sea [the grain connection]. . . . Fat-bellied merchantmen [cargo ships] brought to Piraeus linen and papyrus from Egypt, frankincense [spice] from Syria, dates and wheat flour from Phoenicia, pork and cheese from Syracuse [on the island of Sicily], ivory from Africa, hides and cheeses from Gaul [France] . . . iron ore from Elba [a Mediterranean

island] and the wheat of the Ukraine [the land north of the Black Sea].[78]

Flowing out of Greece at the same time were the silver, olive oil, honey, and pottery of Attica; the copper of Euboea; the horses of Thessaly; the wine, wool, and carpets of Miletus, Chios, Samos, and other poleis of western Asia Minor; and the fine metal artifacts of Corinth and Argos in the Peloponnesus. All of this trade stimulated various business interests and jobs, among which Plato listed "retailers, innkeepers, tax collectors, mines, moneylending, compound interests, and innumerable other things."[79]

The Transporting of Goods and People

The chief means of transportation for traders, merchants, and their goods was ocean shipping. This was because the poor quality of Greek roads, as well as most others

Merchant ships crowd the docks at the Piraeus, Athens's busy port town. Beyond the port, the famous "Long Walls" stretch away toward distant Athens, where the temples on the Acropolis are just barely visible.

in the Mediterranean sphere at the time, made long land trips slow, difficult, and uncomfortable. In the summer the dust on the roadways was often inches deep, and in the winter rains carved out deep ruts. Large rocks and fallen trees were always frequent obstacles. As a result, wagons and mule trains carrying people and products were usually able to travel at no more than an ordinary walking pace, making the transport of most goods by land very expensive.

By contrast, cargo ships could carry larger quantities of goods faster, more easily, and at lower cost. A typical Greek cargo ship was a small bark, or sailing vessel, ranging in length from twenty to sixty feet, with one large rectangular linen sail. Larger, more expensive cargo ships known as *kerkouroi* had oars as well as a sail so that a steady pace could be maintained even when the winds died down. *Kerkouroi* were also equipped with bow rams with which to fight pirate ships. The number of crewmen on a cargo ship varied from one or two to nine or ten, depending on the size of a vessel and its load. Regarding that load, solid goods were stacked in a hold below the deck, while liquids like wine and olive oil were transported in large pottery jars called amphorae.

The lives of traders, traveling merchants, and the sailors who manned the cargo ships were rigorous and sometimes dangerous. In addition to the ever-present threat of pirates, there was the risk of capsizing and sinking. Ship captains usually tried not to sail in bad weather; however, in an age without advanced weather forecasts many ships encountered unexpected storms and ended up on the bottom of the Mediterranean. As an extra precaution, captains tried to sail

As a merchant ship loaded with cargo departs from the Piraeus bound for some foreign port, workers (lower right) prepare to load another vessel.

A two-story inn (right) on the road from Eleusis to Athens. The small, temple-like building (left center) is a "treasury" for storing goods, money, and other valuables.

along coastlines in sight of land. When this was not possible, they prayed for clear skies and navigated by the stars.

The trading life could be lonely, too, for merchants and sailors were often out of touch with family and friends for weeks, months, or even longer. A few tried to keep in contact through letters. A second-century ship captain penned the following note to his brother back in Greece:

Irenaeus to Apollinarius his brother, hearty greetings. I pray always that you may be in health, even as I am in health myself. I wish you to know that I landed on the sixth, and finished unloading on the eighteenth. . . . We are now daily waiting for our clearance papers, but up till today none of us in the grain trade has been released [allowed to leave port]. I greet your wife, also Serenus, and all who love you. Farewell.[80]

Travelers could choose from a wide variety of nightly accommodations on their trips. Those moving overland could stay at small inns on the main roads or, if they preferred to rough it, could sleep in bedrolls in the open. In ports and most cities, travelers were allowed to sleep under the roofed porticoes of stoas and other public buildings. There were also numerous inns and sometimes a few larger, more luxurious hotels called *kata-gogia*. One such hotel, the remains of which have been found at Epidaurus in the Peloponnesus, had 160 rooms arranged around a grid of four wide courtyards.

The Common Trades

The traders, roving merchants, and shippers, of course, constituted only one crucial segment of the commercial business establishment. The tradesmen who actually manufactured the goods constituted another important segment. Local industry varied, but certain trades, listed here by classical scholar H. J. Edwards, were common to most of the larger cities:

> The [building of a] house [employed] quarrymen, brick- and cement-makers, stonemasons . . . bricklayers, foresters, sawyers, carpenters and joiners. . . . The manufacture of furniture and utensils occupied a host of workers in stone, clay, metal, wood, wool, glass, and other substances. . . . The supply of food, drink, and household necessaries occupied flour-merchants, millers, [bread] bakers . . . confectioners [pastry-makers], butchers, fishmongers . . . greengrocers, fruiterers, vintners [wine-makers], salt-boilers . . . cooks, torch-makers. . . . Articles of apparel engaged spinners, weavers, dyers, tailors, fullers [cloth-pressers], cleaners, glovers . . . hatters, tanners [leather-workers] . . . shoemakers. . . . [Transportation needs employed] shipwrights, oar-, sail-, rope-, and tackle-makers, horse-dealers and saddlers, cartwrights [wagon-makers] and wheelwrights.[81]

Among the most common of local Greek industries was bread baking. This tiny clay model depicts four bakers kneading dough while a flute player provides a tune.

The Master Potters

Here, from his scholarly study of the major Greek poleis, The Rise of the Greeks, *historian Michael Grant comments on some of the known masters of the black- and red-figure pottery styles.*

"Two black-figure artists are outstanding. One was the 'Amasis Painter,' . . . [who] was active from ca. 561 to ca. 514 B.C., and during this long period worked on many different scales and a wide variety of subjects. . . . His work is highly finished, and his lithe [agile] figures display a mannered grace, accompanied by touches of vivid, unexpected humor. Meanwhile, during the third quarter of the same century, the different but equally individual Exekias . . . enriched his figures with delicate engraved details. Exekias specialized in scenes loaded with dramatic tension and emotion. . . . The invention of the red-figure style is ascribed to the 'Andocides Painter' (that is to say, one of the painters who worked for the potter Andocides), who was a pupil of . . . Exekias. . . . The 'Andocides Painter' was an artist whose work displays an elegant grace. . . . His figures are drawn on a grand scale, and convey a sense of depth."

Other common tradesmen in the Greek world were sculptors, painters, barbers, perfumers, umbrella makers, goldsmiths and silversmiths, jewelers, bone and ivory carvers, paper and pen makers, florists, musical instrument makers, bird trainers, and toy and doll makers. Almost every such industry had its local masters who employed assistants and apprentices. Many craftsmen formed guilds, or clublike associations, which helped to preserve and keep secret their trade techniques. Men in a guild often socialized and worshiped together and even tended to live in a certain quarter of a city.

Three Essential Industries

Three of the most important local industries, from the standpoint of both their economic impact and the widespread use of the goods they turned out, were pottery making, metal smelting, and silver mining. Describing the potter's art, C. E. Robinson writes:

Modeling was done on a wheel, and it is impossible to exaggerate the beauty of the vessels produced. They were of all shapes and sizes, and for the most part intended for everyday use, such as drinking-cups, mixing-bowls, oil-jars, and so forth. But they were of exquisite design; and there are no more priceless treasures in our modern museums than the Attic, Corinthian, or other Greek vases. When the potter had finished with the vase, it was handed to the painter to adorn. . . . All manner of scenes were depicted; some drawn from mythology, some from everyday life. But such was the imaginative genius of the artists that no two were ever alike. There was no idea of cheap mass-production at Athens.[82]

The two most common pottery styles were "black figure" and "red figure." The first consisted of scenes painted with a glossy black pigment over a reddish-orange background. The other featured the reverse—orange figures and scenes against a black

An amphora, or large jar, made in classical Attica shows artisans working in a bootmaker's shop.

background. The red-figure technique, Michael Grant points out, "provided greater freedom and flexibility, permitting the faithful depiction of muscular structures and ambitious poses, together with varied and realistic details of features and clothing."[83]

The metal smelter turned out all manner of metal goods, ranging from kitchen utensils and lampstands to statues, building tools, and weapons. Bronze, a mixture of copper and tin, was the most common type of metal used. Workers melted the two ores in a brick and clay furnace that reached a temperature of nearly 1100 degrees centigrade. They then poured the liquid metal into molds, which they removed after the bronze cooled. They also made iron artifacts, although these required smelting in larger furnaces that could produce hotter temperatures. When heated, the iron separated from the iron ore, forming a "bloom," or mass of soft metal. The workers then reheated the iron bloom and hammered it into the desired shape.

Because silver was both precious and commonly used to make coins that supported commerce everywhere, silver mining was an important and valuable industry. It was particularly important for Athens, for its silver mines at Laureum were the largest and richest known in the Greek world and helped to support its empire. By the mid-fifth century B.C., as many as twenty thousand slaves toiled at Laureum under horrendous and inhumane conditions. Using hammers and chisels to extract the ore and guided only by the feeble light of small oil lamps, the slaves often had to work lying on their backs for hours in two- or three-foot-high tunnels. Other workers hauled the silver ore in baskets up narrow vertical shafts to the surface.

The unrelenting desire for the wealth and high living standards that silver generated made silver mining a vital growth industry. To ensure a constant supply of the metal, while workers exhausted the ore in one vein, or deposit, others searched for new veins to exploit. Xenophon reported:

> Of all the activities I know, silver mining is the only one in which expansion arouses no envy.... If there are more coppersmiths, for example, copperwork becomes cheap and the coppersmiths retire. The same is true in the iron trade.... But an increase in the amount of silver ore ... brings more people into this industry.[84]

Money, Coins, and Banking

Even though silver and other precious metals were the most valuable commodities, all tradesmen set certain values on their goods. They expected to receive something of equal value in exchange for those goods. In a sense, the glue that held manufacturing, shipping, selling, and the other components of commerce together was this exchange of currency. In the early Archaic Age, the Greeks had no formal money. Instead, they used a barter system in which they exchanged one kind of good for another of similar value. Eventually, the barter system was supplemented, and in some areas replaced, by the exchange of irregularly shaped and heavy lumps of metal, often iron.

Then, in the seventh century B.C. Miletus and other poleis in Asia Minor learned about formal coinage from their eastern neighbors, the Lydians. The idea eventually spread from Miletus to the mainland poleis, among which Athens's neighbor Aegina was the first to issue coins. About 590 B.C., the Aeginetans introduced a silver coin stamped with the image of a turtle. This coin remained the most important in the region until the Athenians issued their silver drachma, stamped with the image of Athena's recognized symbol, the owl. These drachmas, commonly called "owls," became the most common currency in the Mediterranean sphere during the height of the Athenian empire in the fifth century B.C. The only major polis that rejected such coinage was Sparta, which retained the use of heavy metal lumps for currency until the late fourth century B.C.

The Love of Money

Outside of Sparta various other coins besides drachmas became common. There were two-, four-, and ten-drachma pieces, for instance, and also smaller coins called obols, in the ratio of six obols per drachma. It is dif-

ficult to calculate modern equivalents for ancient Greek money. One convenient comparison is the average cost of a bushel of corn and a sheep in the fifth century B.C.—about three and eight drachmas, respectively. In the same age, an average worker made about one drachma per day and a highly skilled artisan about two or three drachmas. A person worth fifty talents, each talent equivalent to six thousand drachmas, was considered very rich.

An Athenian silver drachma, displaying the profile of the goddess Athena on the front and her symbol, the owl, on the back. Appropriately, such coins were often referred to as "owls."

Bankers and Loans

In this excerpt from his article "Commerce and Industry" (in A Companion to Greek Studies), *scholar H. J. Edwards explains some of the practices of the small and financially well-off Greek banking class.*

"Taken as a whole the most important commercial class were the bankers (*trapezitai*), whose functions were threefold: money-changing [converting one form of currency into another], moneylending, and the receipt of deposits for safekeeping. . . . For the business of money-changing . . . a small commission, or agio, was charged. A loan might be friendly [verbal] or formally contracted [written], the latter class being divided according to the security [property put up to secure the loan]. . . . In ordinary loans the commonest standards of interest were 12 and 18 percent per year, payable on the last day of the month to the creditor or his representatives. . . . In the case of a defaulter [borrower who did not pay] the creditor had the right to seize the . . . mortgage on which the loan was secured. . . . Bankers were constantly employed, like our lawyers, as confidential intermediaries [advisors and handlers] . . . in all money matters. Their accounts must have been carefully kept, by themselves and a staff of clerks, chiefly freedmen and slaves: the details [of transactions] would be copied down . . . into day-books and ledgers in which credit and debit accounts were shown on separate pages."

With so much money being exchanged, the development of banking and money lending was inevitable. "The great temples," James and Thorpe write, at first "had a virtual monopoly on banking, starting off by holding valuables on deposit for the wealthy and then moving into moneylending."[85] In time bankers and money changers called *trapezitai*, who maintained tables and booths in the agora, also began lending money. To get a loan, a person pledged something of value, such as land or a house, as security. The banker then lent the person an amount no larger than 50 to 60 percent of the value of the security. If the loan plus interest was not repaid on time, the banker could seize the security. The Greeks had little or no concept of credit, and payments were almost always expected in cash or barter equivalent.

In these and other commercial and business transactions, as in the realm of land ownership, a few fortunate individuals got rich at the expense of the majority who did not. As is still true today, the have-nots envied the haves and often depicted them as greedy. Plato summed up this view in his *Republic*, saying:

The makers of fortunes have a second love of money as a creation of their own, resembling the affection of authors for their poems, or of parents for their children, besides that natural love of it [money], for the sake of use and profit which is common to them and all men. And hence they [the rich] are very bad company, for they can talk about nothing but the praises of wealth.[86]

CHAPTER 6

Gods and Gravestones: Greek Religious Beliefs and Death Rituals

Most Greeks were devoutly religious and their sacred observances and ceremonies were not confined to special days set aside for worship. They had their special religious holidays and festivals, to be sure, but prayer, sacrifice, and other religious ritual influenced, often profoundly, almost every aspect of their everyday lives. For instance, no pious Greek ate a meal without offering a portion of his or her food to the gods. Some sort of sacrifice or prayer regularly preceded all public functions, including court proceedings and meetings of citizen assemblies and councils. And military generals performed a sacrifice before committing their troops to battle. Religious ritual also attended major life-cycle events, such as birth, marriage, and death. Plato summed up the feelings of most of his fellow Greeks when he said, "All men who have any degree of right feeling pray at the beginning of any enterprise great or small."[87]

Origins in the Mists of Time

The exact origins of the Greek religion and its pantheon, or group of gods, is difficult to trace. Some gods, beliefs, and rituals of the Archaic and Classic Ages were apparently very ancient, dating back through the mists of time to the Minoan/Mycenaean era. Other gods and beliefs developed or were borrowed from neighboring west-Asian peoples during the long Greek dark age.

At first, the nature of these religious elements varied significantly from polis to polis. "Just as every little state had its own independent constitution [political set-up]," explains scholar E. A. Gardner, "so also it had its own recognized cycle of gods, and its own manner of worshipping them."[88] In time, certain gods and the mythology, or collection of stories, traditions, and views, surrounding them became more or less universally recognized. This belief system, along with the Greek language, served as an important unifying force. Though each polis always saw itself as a separate nation, common language and religious beliefs instilled the idea that all Greeks were, beneath the political surface, kinsmen.

Most scholars agree that the pantheon worshiped in historic, classical Greece was formalized by about 900 B.C. This is apparently how the classical Greeks themselves saw it. In the fifth century B.C. Herodotus wrote:

> It was only—if I may so put it—the day before yesterday that the Greeks came to know the origin and form of the various gods, and whether or not all of them had always existed; for Homer [in his epic poems the *Iliad* and *Odyssey*] and Hesiod [in his *Theogony*] are the poets who wrote down our religious lore and

A drawing depicting the Greek gods assembled on top of Mt. Olympus. Zeus, the head god, sits on his throne (center) with his wife Hera to his right and Athena (with helmet and spear) directly behind him.

described the gods for us, giving them all their appropriate titles, offices, and powers, and they lived, as I believe, not more than four hundred years ago.[89]

The Greek gods listed and described by Homer and Hesiod were often referred to as the "Olympians" because it was thought that these deities dwelled atop the tallest mountain in Greece, ten-thousand-foot-high Mt. Olympus in Thessaly.

The Greeks saw the Olympians as having human form and also human emotions. The Greek gods made mistakes, fought among themselves, and had marriages, love affairs, and children. Perhaps people found it easier to relate to gods that displayed familiar human qualities. In any case, the often frivolous behavior of the gods was much less important to the Greeks than the power wielded by these deities. The Greek gods, writes C. M. Bowra,

were all to a high degree embodiments of power, whether in the physical world or in the mind of man. From them came literally everything, both visible and invisible, and it was the task of the mortals to make the proper use of what the gods provided. . . . They thought the gods more beautiful than men could ever hope to be, and they did not expect them to follow the rules of human behavior. What counted was their power.[90]

The fifth-century poet Pindar expressed this concept beautifully in his *Odes*: "Single is the race, single of men and of gods; from a single mother we both draw breath. But a difference of power in everything keeps us apart."[91]

The Gods and Their Festivals

That difference of power was most marked in Zeus, who ruled over the other gods. His symbols were the thunderbolt, eagle, and oak tree; and he was married to his sister, Hera, the protector of women, marriage, and childbirth. Often unfaithful to Hera, Zeus had affairs with mortal women, appearing to them in various disguises, including bulls and swans. Zeus's brother Poseidon, whose symbols were the trident, dolphin, and horse, ruled the seas from an underwater palace. Pluto was the god of the Underworld, where it was believed people went when they died. Pluto drove a gold chariot drawn by black horses and owned all of the gold, silver, and precious jewels on the earth. Artemis, write Peach and Millard,

> was the moon goddess. Her silver arrows brought plague and death, though she could heal as well. She protected young girls and pregnant women. Artemis was the mistress of all wild animals and enjoyed hunting in her chariot pulled by stags.[92]

Some of the other important gods were Apollo, Artemis's twin, god of the sun, music, truth, and healing; Ares, god of war, with his symbols the spear and the burning torch; Aphrodite, goddess of love and beauty and often Ares's lover; Dionysus, god of the vine and fertility; Hestia, goddess of the hearth; Demeter, goddess of plants, her symbol a sheaf of wheat; and Athena, Zeus's daughter, goddess of wisdom and war, her symbols the owl and the olive tree.

Although most Greeks recognized and worshiped these and several other gods, individual poleis still retained their own local variations and favorites. Bowra writes:

> Every city was protected by its own special deity who had his or her own temple and festivals. At these festivals, which were still feasts and combined the worship of gods with the gaiety of men, a whole people might feel that it was protected by watchful presences and united in its admiration for them and its sense of belonging to them.[93]

In this way the Athenians recognized Athena as their patron goddess and dedicated their most important religious festival, the *Panathenaea*, to her. Held every four years, it lasted six days and included banquets, athletic contests, music, and dancing. The climax of the celebration was a magnificent procession consisting of thousands of people who marched through the city streets and ended up at the temple complex on the Acropolis.

Other Athenian religious festivals included the *Anthesteria*, held in February, and the City Dionysia, highlighted by the dramatic competitions, in late March. In all, Athens observed about seventy days of religious holidays, and the situation was little different in most other poleis. The Greeks saw these holidays not only as times to honor the gods but also as days of rest. As Plato put it, "The gods, pitying the laborious nature of men, ordained for them, as a rest from their labors, the succession of religious festivals."[94]

Dwellings of the Gods

The traditional customs and physical procedures involved in Greek worship, both during the festivals and at other times, differed in many ways from those of today's major religions. For one thing the Greeks had no sacred religious texts or scriptures comparable to the Christian Bible, Moslem Koran, or Jewish Talmud. The works of Homer and Hesiod, which described the gods and their interactions with humans, were seen simply as important and highly respected literary stories and not as the revealed word or truth of the gods themselves. The Greeks perceived neither the stories about the gods nor the gods themselves as holy or morally perfect. "The Greek sense of the holy," Bowra points out, "was based much less on a feeling of the goodness of the gods than on a devout respect for their incorruptible beauty and unfailing strength."[95] This is confirmed by Plutarch's comment:

> When we consider the three sentiments, admiration, fear, and reverence, which divinity inspires among mankind, we find that men appear to admire the gods and think them blessed because they are immortal and unchangeable; to stand in fear and awe of them because of their . . . authority; and to . . . honor and reverence them because of their justice.[96]

The magnificent Panathenaea *festival reaches its majestic climax before the towering collonade and ornate front pediment of the Parthenon.*

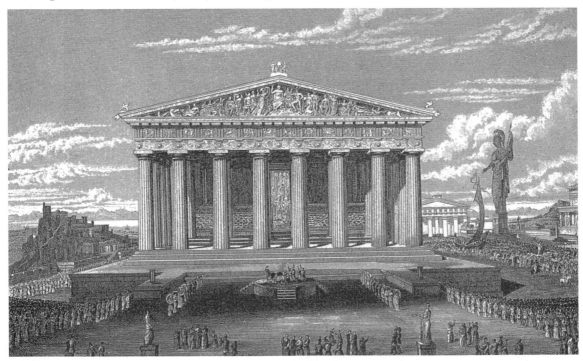

No Love for the Gods

One of the obvious and basic features of most modern religions is a feeling or statement of love for God. But this feature was apparently not part of ancient Greek religious worship. As historian C. M. Bowra comments in his well-known book about the Greeks' unique outlook on life, The Greek Experience:

"Men [in Greece] may respect the gods and make friends of them, but there is nothing that can strictly be called a love of God. . . . If such a relation was missing between gods and men, it lacked divine encouragement between men themselves. The Greeks had their deep affections for family and friends, but these had little support in religion. Zeus was certainly the god of the hearth, of friendship, and of hospitality, but he asked more for loyalty than for love. Indeed, just because the gods personified power, and because this was so strong in local and national allegiances, they could hardly accept so uniting a principle as love. Though the Greeks admired order and sought it everywhere in the scheme of things, they did not see that its most enduring basis is to be found in the affections."

Greek worship also differed in its concept of a church. Unlike a modern church, a temple was not a place in which worshipers assembled for prayer and ritual. John Miliadis explains:

Today the liturgy [ritual] takes place inside the church, for [in it] there is the altar, and there the faithful are assembled. Thus a church is turned inwards, and the form and decoration of the interior are the chief care of the architect. But the altar of an ancient temple was outside, opposite its eastern facade, and there [is where] the sacrifices took place. The temple was simply the dwelling of the god, the sacred shelter of the cult image, and the faithful had very few opportunities for going inside the temple.[97]

A Greek temple was seen as the abode of the god in whose honor it was built. The building contained the image or symbol of the god—for example, the statue of Athena in the cella, or main room, of the Parthenon —and it was thought that the god visited the temple from time to time.

Temples were also storehouses of wealth. Some people donated money and valuables as gifts to a temple's god, while others simply stored their own valuables there for safekeeping, since no one dared to rob such a sacred shrine. In addition, many temples became sanctuaries for oppressed or persecuted individuals. For example, some temples at Ephesus, a polis in Asia Minor, were famous for giving asylum, or protection from capture or prosecution, to runaway slaves.

Sacrifice and Prayer

The altars outside the temples were the locations of actual worship, at least the public version. People also worshiped privately, at the altars in their courtyards, at their hearths, or practically anywhere it was convenient or necessary. The two basic components of worship were sacrifice and prayer. The simplest form of sacrifice, or offering to please a god, was a

libation, a pouring of wine on an altar. All manner of other foods and drinks might be offered, depending on the occasion and the preferences of the god receiving the sacrifice. The kinds of offerings preferred by the various gods were matters of common knowledge.

Among the most common sacrificial offerings were animals, such as goats, sheep, and birds. The ritual of animal sacrifice typically began by draping garlands of flowers over the victim, leading it to the altar, purifying the altar with water, and sprinkling barley grains on and around the victim. Then came the actual sacrifice, in which a worshiper used a club to stun the animal and a knife to cut its throat. The victim's blood drained into a bowl, after which someone sprinkled the

(Above) The giant statue of Zeus designed and executed by Phidias sits in the god's temple at Olympia. (Below) An ancient painting shows worshipers preparing to sacrifice a sheep at an altar.

blood either on the altar or over the worshipers. Finally, the worshipers skinned the animal, cut it up, burned certain portions on the altar to please the god, and then cooked and ate the rest themselves.

During and sometimes before and after the act of sacrifice, worshipers prayed. But prayer was often a separate act, performed before meals, public meetings, athletic contests, and battles, as well as at births, marriages, travel departures, deaths, funerals, and numerous other situations and occasions. According to Gardner:

> The Greek worshiper prayed standing, with his hands raised, palm upwards, to heaven; if he addressed the gods below, he might stretch his arms downward, stamp on the ground to call their attention, or kneel to touch the ground with his hand; but kneeling in prayer, except with this motive, was regarded as barbarian and unworthy of a free man. . . . Prayer was usually made aloud unless there was some special reason for concealment.[98]

People prayed for all manner of things, of course, just as they do today. It was common, for instance, to ask the gods to bestow health, success, riches, or good fortune. A few individuals used prayer in a more noble manner, as evidenced by this prayer attributed to Socrates and addressed to the god Pan, protector of the flocks:

> Beloved Pan, and all you other gods that haunt this place, give me beauty in the inward soul; and may the outward and inward man be at one; May I reckon the wise to be the wealthy, and may I have such a quantity of gold as none but men of moderate strength can carry.[99]

Priests, Oracles, and Mystery Cults

Since any person could pray or sacrifice on his or her own, the Greeks had no priests in the modern sense, that is, full-time, professional spiritual guides. When family members prayed together at home, the head of the household led the ritual. And in large public ceremonies, the leader of a clan, a tribe, or the head of state usually led the ceremony. However, a few religious matters required special skills the average person lacked. For example, the Greeks believed that omens, signs of impending good or bad fortune, could be detected by examining animals' livers, birds' flight formations, and patterns of thunder and lightning. To attend to such matters, each clan usually had its own priest, who inherited his part-time position from a relative.

A much more specialized religious position, one that has no clear modern counterpart, was that of an oracle. Oracles were priestesses who acted as mediums between gods and humans. The way in which oracles were chosen remains unclear, but they were generally peasant women with no special qualifications for the job. People asked an oracle a question, and she gave an answer that was almost always vague and open to interpretation. The trick was to figure out what message the god was trying to convey through the oracle. Various temples throughout Greece had oracles, but the most famous and respected was at the temple of Apollo at Delphi, located just north of the Gulf of Corinth in central Greece. Writes C. E. Robinson:

> Within the temple there is said to have been a chasm [deep pit] through which

Gods and Gravestones: Greek Religious Beliefs and Death Rituals sulphurous fumes issued. Over the chasm was placed a three-legged stool or tripod; and a priestess, seated on the stool, underwent some sort of ecstatic [intensely emotional] frenzy in which she gave inspired utterance to the god's views.[100]

It is likely that oracles took hallucinogenic drugs before or during this ritual. The Roman writer Pliny the Elder described two such drugs, henbane and vervain, in connection with oracles and fortune-tellers. Some evidence suggests that the questioners as well as the oracles may have taken these drugs.

Another very specialized Greek religious ritual that produced an altered mental state was practiced by the mystery cults. These were small, secret sects of worshipers associated with various deities, most often nature or fertility gods. The best known mystery cult was that of the goddess Demeter at Eleusis, in Attica northwest of Athens. Each year in September, new recruits were initiated into the "Eleusian Mysteries." The secret of the initiation rites was very well kept, for to this day no one is sure what went on at these ceremonies. What seems fairly certain, Gardner states, is:

The essential thing in the Mysteries was not the imparting of any doctrine . . . of mystic truth, but the production of a certain mental state, induced by fasting and

The oracle, or priestess, at the Temple of Apollo at Delphi delivers a message from the gods while eager religious pilgrims listen to her revelations.

religious excitement, in which the partaking of the sacred food and drink, the handling of certain sacred objects, and the seeing and hearing of the sacred drama and chants made so great an impression on the excited imagination as to leave a permanent effect on the character [blind devotion to the cult].[101]

Death, Funerals, and the Afterlife

The devout members of mystery cults strongly believed that after death their souls would go to the Elysian Fields, a pleasant, sunlit, and happy portion of Hades, or the Underworld. As is true of nearly all faiths, the Greek religion focused a great deal of attention on death rituals and a belief in an afterlife. The most common belief was that when a person died the god Hermes led his or her soul to the River Styx, which marked the boundary between the world of the living and the Underworld, Pluto's kingdom. Charon, a solemn boatman, ferried the soul across the river. Next, a panel of judges reviewed the soul's earthly life and decided what part of Hades it would end up in. Wicked people's souls were condemned to eternal torment in a ghastly place called Tartarus, while the souls of people who had led virtuous lives went to the Elysian Fields or to an even more beautiful and happy place known as the Islands of the Blessed.

In order to ensure that the soul safely reached the Underworld, a proper funeral was required. The belief was that without a funeral the soul wandered aimlessly along the banks of the River Styx and never gained entry into the Underworld. Thus, funeral rites were handled with the utmost care and reverence. Friends and relatives wore black,

and female relations cut their hair short as a sign of respect. Family members washed the body, dressed it in white, and allowed it to rest at home for a day so that friends and acquaintances could mourn and pay their respects. They also placed an obol in the dead person's mouth, supposedly the fare the soul needed to pay Charon for ferrying it across the River Styx. As to the funeral ceremony itself, scholar J. E. Harrison writes:

On the River Styx, the boatman Charon guides his passengers toward the portal to the Underworld, where Cerebus, the three-headed dog, stands guard.

The body was laid on a bier and borne either on a cart or on the shoulders of friends; hired mourners and flute-players, as well as friends and relations, accompanied it to the grave. The ceremonies at the grave varied . . . [depending on whether] the body was buried or burned. . . . When [it] was burned, a more expensive and tedious process, a pyre [pile of flammable materials] had to be erected; as the fire burned down, wine or water was poured on the ashes to extinguish them, and the bones and ashes . . . were collected in a vase. In the case of burial, as the grave was filled up friends and relations threw in vases, terracotta images and the like, not wholly out of sentiment, but from the fear that the dead man, if not pacified, might return to claim his goods. Save in the case of a public funeral, [there was] no oration nor . . . spoken ritual, but the dead man was thrice saluted by name in a loud voice and the funeral proper was over.[102]

A burial usually took place in a family plot in a cemetery located outside a city's walls. Graves were marked by simple marble

This Athenian grave marker bears a sculpted full-body portrait of the well-to-do woman buried within the accompanying tomb.

Oracles and the Fate of Kingdoms

Greek oracles, like the most famous one at Delphi, regularly dispensed advice and prophecies. Often, oracular statements were trivial and affected only the life, relationships, and fortunes of a pilgrim who journeyed to the shrine and asked a question. Occasionally, however, the words of an oracle affected or foretold the fate of an entire polis, a kingdom, or a people. One of the most famous examples occurred in 546 B.C. as the Persians were about to invade Lydia, a kingdom encompassing most of Asia Minor. The Lydian king, Croesus, sent a messenger to Delphi to consult the oracle of Apollo about whether it was wise to fight the Persians. The oracle stated that if Croesus crossed the Halys River and attacked the invaders, he would destroy a great empire. Filled with confidence, Croesus attacked, but to his surprise he met defeat and ruin. He had forgotten that the oracle often couched its advice in the form of a riddle and in this case the kingdom that was destroyed was his own.

The Delphic oracle gave another fateful piece of advice in 630 B.C. to the residents of the Aegean island polis of Thera, which was in the throes of a devastating famine. The oracle instructed the Therans to abandon their home and establish a colony on the northern coast of Africa. Some of the people followed this advice, and the new colony became very prosperous.

A third well-known example of momentous oracular prophecy occurred in 480 B.C. when the Persians were invading mainland Greece. Athenian leaders consulted the Delphic oracle, who said that Greece's only hope lay in the defense provided by its "wooden wall." Some people thought this meant that they should build walls of wood around their cities. The shrewd leader Themistocles, however, decided that the oracle was referring to a fleet of wooden ships. He quickly marshaled the Greek naval forces and crushed the Persians in the great sea battle of Salamis.

---

columns or slabs or, when a family could afford it, elaborate stone coffins and crypts adorned with carved portraits of the dead person. For weeks after a funeral, female relatives brought offerings of perfume and other liquids in pottery containers called *lekythoi*.

Like people of all times and places, the Greeks feared death, partly because, despite the teachings of the faith, there was never any visible, tangible proof of an afterlife. But their religion advocated that death, whatever it had in store, was a natural part of the scheme of things. In this view, death was another step or milestone in nature's regular and eternal life cycle. Therefore, though in some ways mysterious and terrifying, death must be ultimately beneficial. Plato put it this way:

> Death is good, for one of two reasons: either death is a state of nothingness and utter unconsciousness, or, as men say, there is a migration of the soul from this world to another. Now if you suppose that there is no consciousness, but an undisturbed sleep, death will be an unspeakable gain. But if death is the journey to another place, what good can be greater than this?[103]

Mind and Body: Pursuing the Physical and Intellectual Ideal

Perhaps the finest and most unique Greek cultural ideal, one many later societies greatly admired and attempted to imitate, was the harmonious blend of physical and mental achievement. On the one hand was the development of the body. Comments Rodney Castleden:

> In classical Greece an ideal of human physical perfection was held up for admiration, and for a particular purpose; the city-state needed strong young men to defend and preserve it, so there was a strong practical need to encourage the development of strong, healthy male bodies.[104]

On the other hand was the development of the mind, which could and should be used to develop a better understanding of the natural world and humanity's place within it. The Greeks, writes C. M. Bowra, had an overwhelming desire "to understand things more exactly, to penetrate the mystery which enveloped them, to explain them in rational language, and to find rules and principles in nature."[105]

In ancient Greece these two ideals were not seen as separate goals; they glorified the concept of a keen mind in a strong, athletic body. The stereotypes of the dim-witted sports hero and the soft, flabby intellectual were alien and repulsive to most Greeks. A hint of how deeply this idea was ingrained in the popular consciousness can be seen in the common Greek description of a socially backward individual: "He can neither swim nor spell." The degree of a person's combined physical and mental development, then, helped to define that person's perceived worth as an individual.

Though not every Greek man and woman was physically and mentally equipped to achieve the mind-body ideal, the fact that so many wanted and tried to achieve it strongly influenced the social customs and institutions of most poleis. Athletic training and sports contests became an integral part of everyday life, from early childhood education to mature adulthood. And parents, extended family, schools, gymnasiums, and social mores often combined to instill and promote a thirst for literacy, knowledge, and understanding that stayed with a person for life. The Greeks introduced the Olympic athletic spirit that survives today on a global scale and invented the intellectual disciplines of science and philosophy that have profoundly shaped our civilization.

The Games at Olympia

The Greek love of sports and athletic competitions was apparently very ancient. In the *Iliad*, which describes the exploits of the Mycenaean Greeks before the dark age, Homer described athletic contests that included running, wrestling, boxing, and chariot racing. The exact way that athletic traditions subsequently developed is unknown. What is certain is that sports contests within and among poleis became a regular feature of many important religious festivals. As the Quennells explain:

> Like every other Greek activity the games were held under the patronage of the gods, and after sacrifice had been made to them. Fundamentally, the games kept men fit and prepared them for war; also they satisfied the Greek ideal—that

a healthy body was necessary for a well-balanced mind. The Greeks, being artists, must have derived great pleasure from watching beautifully proportioned bodies in action.[106]

The most important and famous of these festival games was that of Olympian Zeus, held every four years at Olympia in the western Peloponnesus. Beginning in 776 B.C., athletes from all over the Greek world converged every fourth summer on Olympia for what became known as the Olympic games. So momentous and honored were these games that even in times of war the combatants temporarily laid down their arms to compete

Young Greek men exercise and play sports at a gymnasium. The two at lower left are in the final stages of a boxing match. At the time, boxers continued to fight even after one athlete went down.

in peace. In his *First Olympian Ode*, Pindar wrote, "If, my soul, you yearn to celebrate great games, look no further for another star shining . . . brighter than the sun, or for a contest mightier than Olympia."[107]

The Olympic contests were open only to men and boys. In fact, for a long time women were not allowed to attend the games even as spectators, probably because their husbands and brothers feared they might be corrupted by the crowds of strange men. So women had their own games, the *Heraia*, held every four years in honor of the goddess Hera. Consisting of three footraces for girls of different ages, the *Heraia* was minor in scope and importance compared to the men's Olympics.

At first the Olympic games consisted of only a few events, but more were added over time. By the fifth century B.C., the games lasted five days. On the first day the athletes and tens of thousands of spectators worshiped and sacrificed at the altars outside of the temple of Olympian Zeus. Inside the temple cella stood a magnificent forty-three-foot-tall statue of the god that later became known as one of the "seven wonders of the ancient world." The second day was devoted to the "junior" competitions, in which boys engaged in wrestling, boxing, and various footraces and horse races.

On the third day, the contests for adult men began. They consisted of a number of footraces, one performed in full battle armor, along with wrestling, boxing, and the *pankration*. The latter was an exciting and extremely popular combination of wrestling, boxing, and street fighting. Writes C. E. Robinson:

This Greek vase painting shows two boxers (left) and two runners. Such athletes most often competed naked, as shown.

A scene from a chariot race at Olympia. Unlike later such races staged in Roman "circuses," the Greek versions featured no intentional brutality and as a result few drivers died.

In this very brutal form of sport any means of vanquishing an opponent were permitted, except biting or gouging out his eyes. So fierce was the struggle that sometimes men were killed; and the story is told of one particular *pankratist* who allowed himself to be strangled rather than lift the finger which gave admission of defeat.[108]

The fourth day of the games witnessed the pentathlon, a series of five events that included the javelin throw, discus throw, long jump, two-hundred-yard sprint, and a wrestling bout. Horse races and chariot races also occurred on the fourth day. These events would appear very familiar to modern ath-

letes and sports fans. However, as James and Thorpe point out:

Two features of the ancient Olympics would undoubtedly deter modern athletes. The first is the shape of the track. We are used to one made up of two straights joined together by curves, with a large open area in the middle for field events. The Greek stadium was a rectangle about two-hundred yards long and twenty-five to forty yards wide with a starting line at each end and a turning post in the middle of each line. In longer races the . . . runners had to make for the post and run around it, which must have led to some real scrambles. The second

Divine Olympia

In this excerpt from his Atlas of the Greek World, *scholar Peter Levi describes the area where Olympia was located and some of its remains.*

"Olympia was a sanctuary, a sacred wood called Altis, in the unpoliticized [politically neutral] countryside of western south Greece [in the Peloponnesus], on the banks of the powerful river Alpheios. It was named for the Olympian gods, and the hill that overlooked it belonged [it was believed] to Kronos, father of Zeus, and perhaps to his mother. By the 8th century [B.C.] Olympia had become an immensely rich and powerful holy place and the center of an international Greek festival of athletic games. The sanctuary has been painfully reconstructed fragment by fragment from the mud of the Alpheios floods which buried it. The altar of Zeus was made of ashes, and it was utterly dissolved [in the floods]. But his temple, built in the 5th century [B.C.], has survived in colossal ruins. There were cults of heroes, legendary human beings of divine ancestry, as well as of gods at Olympia; in the end the athletes themselves came to seem half-divine."

These ruined columns are all that is left of one of the magnificent structures adjoining the athletic stadium at Olympia.

feature is the fact that the athletes competed naked. Tradition has it that [in the dim past] a runner's shorts slipped down; he tripped over them and was killed, with the result that the [officials] banned the wearing of shorts.[109]

Exercise an Essential Part of Life

On the fifth and final day of the Olympic games, the crowds gathered to see the crowning of the victors, who each received a wreath of olive leaves. The most honored victors of ancient times were Leonidas of Rhodes, who won twelve victories in four successive games between 164 and 152 B.C.; and Milo of Chroton, who won the wrestling competition six times between 540 and 520 B.C. These and other winners became, in a very real sense, national heroes. On returning to his polis, an Olympic champion was honored with parties and celebrations, received numerous awards and gifts, and often was provided with free meals for the rest of his life. "The glory of the Olympiads," wrote Pindar, "shoots its rays afar in his races, where speed and strength are matched in the bruise of toil. But the victor, for the rest of his life, enjoys days of contentment."[110]

With such potential for glory, both for the athlete and his home city, it is not surprising that athletics and the cultivation of sports stars became a major institution in most poleis. City governments sponsored talented young athletes and paid them well, introducing the idea of professional sports. Over the centuries, some Greeks criticized this element of professionalism, saying that greed for money, prestige, and other rewards had corrupted the games. They preferred the more traditional and "purer" amateur athlete who competed solely for the "glory of sport." It was this Greek amateur athletic ideal that inspired a Frenchman, Baron Coubertin, to organize the first modern Olympic games in 1896.

Yet the Greeks' glorification and sponsorship of sports heroes had a beneficial side effect in the community. The importance placed on the Olympics and other important athletic contests strongly promoted the ideas of friendly competition and regular exercise, or *gymnastiki*, for physical conditioning and good health. According to E. A. Gardner:

> Physical exercise was an essential part of the life of all free Greeks and to it a considerable part of the day was devoted. It

The victor of an Olympic event is crowned with a wreath of olive leaves. He will be worshiped as a hero for the rest of his life.

A huge crowd converges on the stadium at the first modern Olympic games held in Athens in 1896.

took place for the most part in . . . gymnasiums (or gymnasia), which were originally of a simple character, but grew in luxury and splendor until they became . . . elaborate structures.[111]

A typical gym consisted not only of a building with rooms for changing, bathing, and socializing, but also of an adjacent field for exercising and playing sports. Before going out onto the field, a person stripped naked and rubbed oil over his body, partly for protection from the hot sun.

Once on the field, gym patrons could choose from a wide variety of physical activities. Those few who preferred to exercise alone could run on a course covered with soft sand, throw the javelin or discus, or broad jump while holding heavy weights. But most chose group activities. These included games that resembled tennis and field hockey, as well as ball throwing, wrestling, and a vigorous kind of regimented dancing. Boxing was also popular, although in the gym it tended to be less strenuous and brutal than in public competitions. The boxers wore padded caps and gloves for protection.

After completing their workouts, patrons used the public baths and showers at the gym. Although women usually were not allowed on the exercise field, some gyms offered female shower facilities. Both male and female bathers generally paid a small token fee to the attendant who kept the facilities clean.

Knowledge for Its Own Sake

Keeping the body in tip-top shape fulfilled only half of the mind-body ideal. The fact

The Wisest of Men

The fifth-century B.C. Athenian philosopher Socrates possessed one of the greatest minds in history. In Books That Changed the World, *scholar Robert Downs wrote that Socrates*

"bequeathed [left] not one line of writing to posterity, but [his] thoughts, as recorded and interpreted by Plato, have left a profound impress upon all succeeding generations. Plato was about twenty when he met Socrates, and he became his ardent disciple for the remaining seven or eight years of the sage's life. Socrates was a strange, uncouth figure . . . wandering about the city barefoot and poor, said to be neglectful of his wife and children and given to endless argumentation."

Uncouth or not, Socrates attracted a loyal following of young Greek intellectuals. Using his famous "Socratic method"— teaching by asking his students questions and encouraging them to find the answers on their own—Socrates preached that goodness stems from knowledge about one's self and the world and that evil and wickedness are the result of ignorance. In his Symposium, *Xenophon recalled that his mentor was*

"so just that he wronged no man in the most trifling affair . . . so wise that he never erred in distinguishing better from worse . . . so capable of discerning the character of others, and of [teaching] them virtue and honor, that he seemed to be such as the best and happiest of men would be."

Even more moving was this simple memorial from Plato's Phaedo:

"My friend Socrates . . . I may truly call the wisest, and justest, and best of all men whom I have ever known."

that the Greeks considered mental and physical development equally important is illustrated by the dual nature of their gymnasiums. Many housed small libraries and reading rooms. In the fifth century B.C., the gym also became a favorite forum and lecture hall for teacher-thinkers called philosophers, at the time a uniquely Greek phenomenon. The term *philosophy* is a combination of the Greek words *philo*, "love," and *sophia*, which meant "knowledge" as well as wisdom. Thus a philosopher was one who loved knowledge.

The philosophers, who usually referred to themselves as *sophoi*, or sages, aimed to understand the true nature of the world and the physical and moral position of human beings within it. For example, the first true philosopher, Thales, born in Miletus in the seventh century B.C., sought to find a *physis*, or single and simple underlying principle, that made the universe work. According to Michael Grant:

Thales of Miletus, the first widely recognized Greek philosopher.

The simplicity of Thales's insistence on a single unifying principle in the physical world, despite all appearances to the contrary . . . established a new and fruitful epoch in Greek thought. . . . Thales was able to . . . ask questions about [highly generalized concepts] and seek rational answers to the questions he had asked. That is to say . . . he was capable of aiming at the pursuit of knowledge for its own sake, by means of abstract reasoning combined with the use of the eye and mind.[112]

In pursuing knowledge for its own sake and attempting a systematic, organized approach to learning, Thales was also the first scientist. For a long time the Greeks did not draw a clear distinction between philosophy and science, which they called *episteme*.

The philosophers not only pursued knowledge and the meaning of life but also shared both their knowledge and their passion for learning with their fellow citizens. Young men might sit for hours in the courtyard of a gym listening to and asking questions of a respected sage. The outstanding sage of the fifth century B.C. was Socrates. As scholar Robert B. Downs tells it:

The magic of the master teacher's words affected all hearers. Feigning [pretending] ignorance, Socrates did not profess to know or teach anything. Instead he induced everyone who approached him to give an account of his soul and to

This drawing depicts the teacher/philosopher Socrates asking and answering questions, probably in the Stoa of the Athenian agora.

defend his views and opinions in the light of reason. His technique invariably was to ask a series of searching questions— queries that explored men's innermost thoughts, stimulated the mental processes of the young men by whom he was constantly surrounded, and exposed the pretensions [arrogance] of pompous citizens who claimed superior knowledge.[113]

Thus, gymnasiums came to resemble informal community colleges. A few outstanding individuals sought to formalize the concept, most notably Plato, who founded the Academy in 387 B.C., and his pupil Aristotle, who established the Lyceum in 335 B.C., both in Athens. These schools, devoted to research and instruction in philosophy and science, were housed in functioning gymnasiums where students exercised their bodies as well as their minds.

Teachers and Schools

As the demand for learning and new knowledge grew rapidly in most Greek poleis, another kind of teacher, the sophist, or "wisdom-seller," became popular. Sophists traveled from place to place offering their services as tutors and lecturers. Unlike Socrates, Plato, and other philosophers, the sophists charged money for dispensing knowledge. The sophists taught grammar, mathematics, and geography, but most especially rhetoric, or public speaking. Robinson points out:

It was a time when men were anxious to make their way in the world; and since politics and the law courts seemed to afford the easiest way of attaining prominence, it was obvious that a training in oratory was the best passport to success. Sophists taught men how to adorn their speeches with elegant phrases, how to work on the feelings of a jury or a mob, and above all how to argue a point. They were not very particular about the truth or falsehood of the arguments they used.[114]

This apparent callous disregard for the truth bothered philosophers such as Plato and Aristotle, for whom the search for the truth in all things was paramount. They also objected to the buying and selling of knowledge, which they saw as undignified. "The art of the sophist," said Aristotle, "is to appear to be wise without really being so; and the sophist makes money from a feigned wisdom."[115] Plato was even more direct, remarking "Sophistry is a hunt after the souls of rich young men of good repute."[116] These criticisms seem a bit harsh to us today, in an age when it is perfectly acceptable for a person to make a living from teaching. The concept of the professional teacher is the chief legacy of the sophists.

Both the philosophers and the sophists, of course, operated in the realm of "higher learning," which served young adults and up. But in all poleis young children received some kind of formal or informal education. Young girls, for example, received instruction at home from their mothers or from hired tutors. Beginning at age six, young boys usually attended a series of three privately run community schools, which strongly promoted the Greek mind-body ideal.

The first kind of boys' school was run by teachers called *grammatistes*, who taught reading, writing, and simple mathematics. In the second school, a boy learned music and poetry from teachers known as *kitharistes*. Here, students received instruction in play-

Spartan youths receive instruction in dancing and the use of weapons in the dromos, *or public walkway of their polis.*

ing the lyre, and perhaps other instruments, and were expected to memorize long passages of the national epic poems, Homer's *Iliad* and *Odyssey*. In the third school, teachers called *paidotribes* gave instruction in dancing and athletics. It was common for a *paidotribe* to take his students on outings to *palaistra*, schools that specialized in teaching young men how to wrestle. Wealthier families often hired a slave or freedman called a *paidagogos* to escort a boy to school and supervise his behavior during school hours.

The main exception to this educational approach was in Sparta where youthful learning, like most other social activities, was controlled and directed by the strict *agoge* military system. Explain Peach and Millard:

> Spartan schooling emphasized physical fitness. The most important subjects were athletics, dancing, and weapon training. Pupils were also taught music and patriotic songs, Spartan law, and some poetry.

However, these more academic subjects were not considered important, as the aim of the Spartan system was to produce tough, healthy adults who would become warriors and mothers of warriors.[117]

The Greek Spirit

Outside of Sparta, in most of the rest of Greece the pursuit of learning and knowledge continually bore extraordinary fruit. Widespread early childhood education, coupled with the higher learning of the sophists and philosophers, produced the world's first society in which a majority of people were literate and educated. The result of this stress on developing the human intellect was an explosion of literary, philosophical, and scientific achievement: the penetrating observations of human nature by Socrates, Aristotle, and Plato; the magnificent dramas of Aeschylus, Sophocles, and their colleagues; the mov-

Things Are Numbers

Pythagoras, one of the founders of the science of mathematics, was born on the Aegean island of Samos in 580 B.C. In this excerpt from his book A History of Knowledge, *scholar Charles Van Doren tells how the Greek thinker discovered the existence of a relationship between abstract numbers and material objects.*

"Pythagoras is . . . the apparent inventor of the idea of the music of the spheres, which was in line with his general thinking about mathematics. One day, the legend goes, while sitting with a musical instrument in his lap, Pythagoras suddenly realized that the divisions of a taut string that produced its harmonies could be described in terms of simple ratios between pairs of numbers, to wit, 1 to 2, 2 to 3, and 3 to 4. We now write these ratios as 1/2, 2/3, and 3/4. This extraordinary fact astonished Pythagoras, who loved music, for it seemed to him exceedingly strange that there should be a connection between numbers, on the one hand, and the notes of a string, on the other, which could move a listener to tears or exalt his spirit. As he reflected on this strange relationship, Pythagoras began to feel that numbers might have an even greater influence on material things. He and his disciples soon arrived at the conclusion that things *are* numbers and numbers *are* things. Thus was discovered the intimate connection between mathematics and the material world that has both inspired and puzzled thinkers since this day."

ing lyrics of Pindar and other master poets; the works of Herodotus, Thucydides, and Xenophon, the world's first historians; the brilliant mathematical theorems of Pythagoras and Euclid; Democritus's and Leucippus's theory of atoms; the medical advances and doctor's oath of Hippocrates; Aristarchus's realization that the earth revolves around the sun; Anaximander's ideas foreshadowing the theory of evolution; and the fabulous inventions of Archimedes, including giant cranes that could lift huge ships out of the water.

These and many other notable achievements of the Greeks grew out of their spirit of eternal questioning and their drive to examine and understand every facet of life and the world. Their achievements and their questioning spirit became a legacy that has thrilled, fascinated, and profoundly influenced the world ever since. The Greeks, comments noted scholar Charles Van Doren,

set off on intellectual craft to explore unknown seas of thought. With their unprecedented and inexplicable genius they undertook this adventure, over and over, for nearly a thousand years. . . . In so doing they set before the human race an image of what it might become.[118]

The Greeks' urge to know, to learn, and to discover the truth, which later societies so admired and strove to imitate, was the product of their unique social ideas, customs, and institutions. Therefore, what they did in their everyday lives indirectly affected humanity's future. Their society and their ways were certainly not perfect, but their special spirit has shaped the intellectual course of Western civilization more than that of any other single people in history. And for that, we and our descendants must stand forever in their debt.

Notes

Introduction: Striving for the Good Life

1. Ariphron, *Hymn to Health*, quoted in C. M. Bowra, *The Greek Experience*. New York: New American Library, 1957.
2. Bowra, *The Greek Experience*.
3. Charles B. Gulick, *Modern Traits in Old Greek Life*. New York: Cooper Square Publishers, 1963.
4. Plato, *Laws*, in *Dialogues*. Translated by Benjamin Jowett. New York: Random House, 1937.
5. Heraclitus, quoted in J. Burnet, ed., *Early Greek Philosophy*. London: A. and C. Black, 1930.
6. Sophocles, *Antigone*, in Bernard Knox, ed., *The Norton Book of Classical Literature*. New York: W. W. Norton, 1993.

Chapter 1: Citizens and Slaves: The People of the Greek City-State

7. Rodney Castleden, *Minoans: Life in Bronze Age Crete*. New York: Routledge, 1990.
8. Bowra, *The Greek Experience*.
9. Pericles, *Funeral Oration*, quoted in Thucydides, *The Peloponnesian Wars*. Translated by Benjamin Jowett. New York: Washington Square Press, 1963.
10. Michael Grant, *The Rise of the Greeks*. New York: Macmillan, 1987.
11. Herodotus, *The Histories*. Translated by Aubrey de Sélincourt. New York: Penguin Books, 1972.
12. Quoted in C. E. Robinson, *Everyday Life in Ancient Greece*. Oxford, England: Clarendon Press, 1968.
13. Robinson, *Everyday Life in Ancient Greece*.
14. Grant, *The Rise of the Greeks*.
15. Michael Grant, *A Social History of Greece and Rome*. New York: Charles Scribner's Sons, 1992.
16. Gulick, *Modern Traits in Old Greek Life*.
17. Sophocles, *Ajax*, in Whitney J. Oates and Eugene O'Neill Jr., eds., *The Complete Greek Drama*. New York: Random House, 1938.
18. Pericles, *Funeral Oration*, in Thucydides, *The Peloponnesian Wars*.
19. Grant, *The Rise of the Greeks*.
20. Robinson, *Everyday Life in Ancient Greece*.
21. Grant, *A Social History of Greece and Rome*.
22. Aristotle, *Politics*, in Robert M. Hutchins, ed., *The Works of Aristotle*. Chicago: Encyclopaedia Britannica, 1952.
23. Susan Peach and Anne Millard, *The Greeks*. London: Usborne, 1990.
24. Robinson, *Everyday Life in Ancient Greece*.
25. Grant, *The Rise of the Greeks*.
26. Pierre Léveque, *The Birth of Greece*. New York: Harry N. Abrams, 1994.

Chapter 2: Country Versus City: Contrasting but Interdependent Lifestyles

27. Aristophanes, *Clouds*, in Moses Hadas, ed., *The Complete Plays of Aristophanes*. New York: Bantam Books, 1962.

28. Robinson, *Everyday Life in Ancient Greece*.
29. Aristotle, *On Longevity and Shortness of Life*, in Robert M. Hutchins, ed., *The Works of Aristotle*.
30. Hesiod, *Works and Days*, in *The Works of Hesiod*. Translated by H. C. Evelyn-White. Cambridge, MA: Harvard University Press, 1914.
31. Herodotus, *The Histories*.
32. Aristotle, *Economics*, in W. D. Ross, ed., *The Works of Aristotle*. Oxford, England: Clarendon Press, 1921.
33. Theognis, quoted in *Greek Lyrics*. Translated by Richard Lattimore. Chicago: University of Chicago Press, 1960.
34. Marjorie Quennell and C. H. B. Quennell, *Everyday Things in Ancient Greece*. New York: G. P. Putnam's Sons, 1968.
35. Robinson, *Everyday Life in Ancient Greece*.
36. Thomas Craven, *The Pocket Book of Greek Art*. New York: Pocket Books, 1950.
37. Craven, *The Pocket Book of Greek Art*.
38. Quoted in Peter Green, *The Parthenon*. New York: Newsweek Book Division, 1973.
39. John Miliadis, *The Acropolis*. Athens: M. Pechlivanidis, no date given.
40. Plutarch, *Pericles*, in *The Rise and Fall of Athens: Nine Greek Lives*. Translated by Ian Scott-Kilvert. New York: Penguin Books, 1960.
41. Léveque, *The Birth of Greece*.
42. Plutarch, *Pericles*.
43. Pericles, *Funeral Oration*, in Thucydides, *The Peloponnesian Wars*.

Chapter 3: Houses and Their Contents: How a Greek Home Operated

44. Plato, *Statesman*, in *Dialogues*.
45. Ian Jenkins, *Greek and Roman Life*.

Cambridge, MA: Harvard University Press, 1986.
46. Gulick, *Modern Traits in Old Greek Life*.
47. Quoted in Gulick, *Modern Traits in Old Greek Life*.
48. Peter James and Nick Thorpe, *Ancient Inventions*. New York: Ballantine Books, 1994.
49. Gulick, *Modern Traits in Old Greek Life*.
50. James and Thorpe, *Ancient Inventions*.
51. Gulick, *Modern Traits in Old Greek Life*.
52. Quoted in Gulick, *Modern Traits in Old Greek Life*.
53. James and Thorpe, *Ancient Inventions*.
54. Robinson, *Everyday Life in Ancient Greece*.
55. Cornelius Nepos, *The Book of the Great Generals of Foreign Nations*. Translated by John C. Rolfe. Cambridge, MA: Harvard University Press, 1960.
56. Lysias, *Speeches*. Translated by W. R. M. Lamb. Cambridge, MA: Harvard University Press, 1930.
57. Xenophon, *Oeconomicus*. Translated by E. C. Marchant et al., in *Xenophon in Seven Volumes*. Cambridge, MA: Harvard University Press, 1921.
58. Plato, *Symposium*. Translated by Tom Griffith. Berkeley: University of California Press, 1989.

Chapter 4: Social Customs and Entertainment: The Pursuit of Leisure

59. Aristophanes, *Peace*, in Hadas, *The Complete Plays of Aristophanes*.
60. Jenkins, *Greek and Roman Life*.
61. Gulick, *Modern Traits in Old Greek Life*.

62. Peach and Millard, *The Greeks.*
63. Menander, from an unidentified play, quoted in *The Norton Book of Classical Literature.*
64. Theognis, quoted in *Greek Lyrics.*
65. Menander, *The Grouch*, in Lionel Casson, ed., *Masters of Ancient Comedy.* New York: Macmillan, 1960.
66. Jenkins, *Greek and Roman Life.*
67. Plutarch, *Life of Lycurgus*, in *Lives of the Noble Grecians and Romans.* Translated by John Dryden. Chicago: Encyclopaedia Britannica, 1952.
68. Quoted in Robinson, *Everyday Life in Ancient Greece.*
69. Edith Hamilton, *The Greek Way to Western Civilization.* New York: New American Library, 1942.
70. James and Thorpe, *Ancient Inventions.*
71. Paul Roche, "The Message of Aeschylus," in *The Orestes Plays of Aeschylus.* New York: New American Library, 1962.
72. Hamilton, *The Greek Way.*
73. James H. Butler, *The Theater and Drama of Greece and Rome.* San Franciso: Chandler Publishing, 1972.
74. Lysias, *Speeches.*

Chapter 5: Business and Commerce: How Goods Were Made, Shipped, and Sold

75. Gulick, *Modern Traits in Old Greek Life.*
76. Gulick, *Modern Traits in Old Greek Life.*
77. Léveque, *The Birth of Greece.*
78. W. G. Hardy, *The Greek and Roman World.* Cambridge, MA: Schenkman, 1962.
79. Plato, *Laws.*
80. Quoted in Gulick, *Modern Traits in Old Greek Life.*
81. H. J. Edwards, "Commerce and Industry," in Leonard Whibley, ed., *A Companion to Greek Studies.* New York: Hafner Publishing, 1963.
82. Robinson, *Everyday Life in Ancient Greece.*
83. Grant, *The Rise of the Greeks.*
84. Xenophon, *Poroi*, quoted in M. I. Finley, *The Ancient Economy.* Berkeley: University of California Press, 1985.
85. James and Thorpe, *Ancient Inventions.*
86. Plato, *Republic.* Translated by F. M. Cornford. New York: Oxford University Press, 1945.

Chapter 6: Gods and Gravestones: Greek Religious Beliefs and Death Rituals

87. Plato, *Timaeus*, in *Dialogues.*
88. E. A. Gardner, "Mythology and Religion," in *A Companion to Greek Studies.*
89. Herodotus, *The Histories.*
90. Bowra, *The Greek Experience.*
91. Pindar, *Odes*, in *The Odes of Pindar.* Translated by Richard Lattimore. Chicago: University of Chicago Press, 1976.
92. Peach and Millard, *The Greeks.*
93. Bowra, *The Greek Experience.*
94. Plato. *Laws.*
95. Bowra, *The Greek Experience.*
96. Plutarch, *Aristides*, in *The Rise and Fall of Athens: Nine Greek Lives.*
97. Miliadis, *The Acropolis.*
98. Gardner, "Mythology and Religion."
99. Quoted in Plato, *Phaedrus*, in *Dialogues.*
100. Robinson, *Everyday Life in Ancient Greece.*
101. Gardner, "Mythology and Religion."
102. J. E. Harrison, "Rituals of Birth, Marriage, and Death," in *A Companion to Greek Studies.*
103. Plato, *Apology*, in *Dialogues.*

Chapter 7: Mind and Body: Pursuing the Physical and Intellectual Ideal

104. Castleden, *Minoans*.
105. Bowra, *The Greek Experience*.
106. Quennells, *Everyday Things in Ancient Greece*.
107. Pindar, *First Olympian Ode*, in *The Odes of Pindar*.
108. Robinson, *Everyday Life in Ancient Greece*.
109. James and Thorpe, *Ancient Inventions*.
110. Pindar, *First Olympian Ode*, in *The Odes of Pindar*.
111. E. A. Gardner, "Exercise, Games, Baths," in *A Companion to Greek Studies*.
112. Grant, *The Rise of the Greeks*.
113. Robert B. Downs, *Books That Changed the World*. New York: Penguin Books, 1983.
114. Robinson, *Everyday Life in Ancient Greece*.
115. Aristotle, *Sophistical Refutations*, in Ross, *The Works of Aristotle*.
116. Plato, *Sophist*, in *Dialogues*.
117. Peach and Millard, *The Greeks*.
118. Charles Van Doren, *A History of Knowledge: Past, Present, and Future*. New York: Ballantine Books, 1991.

Glossary

acropolis: "High place of the city"; in a Greek polis, a central hill or cliff used for defensive and ceremonial purposes.

agio: A small commission charged by money changers.

agora: The main marketplace of a polis.

agoge: Sparta's rigid military system.

agoranomoi: Public officials who inspected goods sold in the Athenian marketplace.

amphorae: Large pottery jars for storing wine, olive oil, and other liquids.

andron: A room in which the master of a house dined and entertained guests.

Anthesteria: An Athenian religious festival honoring the god Dionysus.

apella: In Sparta, an assembly of citizens over the age of thirty.

Archaic Age: In Greece, the historical period lasting from about 800 to 500 B.C.

archon: In Athens, an elected government administrator.

arete: A person's natural or inborn capacity or potential.

aristoi: "Best people"; aristocrats.

Attica: The peninsula on the eastern Greek coast on which Athens is located.

bailiff: An overseer who ran a country farm or estate for the well-to-do owner who resided in the city.

black-figure: A pottery style in which the figures and scenes on the artifacts are black against an orange background.

Boule: In Athens, the Council, or legislative body that formulated laws and state policy.

brazier: A metal container in which charcoal was burned to provide interior heating.

bronze: A mixture of the metals copper and tin.

Bronze Age: In Greece, the historical period lasting from about 3000 to 1100 B.C., characterized by the use of bronze weapons and artifacts.

candelabra: Multiple-candle holders.

capital: The top of a column.

cella: The main room of a Greek temple, usually housing the cult image, or statue, of a god.

chamber pot: A container in which people deposited their personal sewage and later dumped into the streets.

chiton: A basic tunic, worn by both men and women.

chlamys: An outer cloak fastened at one shoulder by a brooch or pin, worn mostly by young men and soldiers.

choregus: A wealthy backer of plays and other theatrical events.

chorus: In the theater, a group of actors who usually spoke and moved in unison and who interacted with the main characters.

City Dionysia: A lavish yearly Athenian religious festival honoring the god Dionysus; also, the dramatic contests that took place during the festival.

Classic Age: In Greece, the historical period lasting from about 500 to 300 B.C., in which Greek civilization reached its zenith.

colonnade: A row of columns.

cottabos: A party game in which drinkers tried to hit a target with the wine dregs left in their cups.

deme: In ancient Athenian Attica, a small local community.

demos: The people.

Dorians: Warlike Europeans who overran and devastated Greece in about 1100 B.C., initiating a cultural dark age.

drachma: A silver coin issued by Athens and other poleis.

drum: A single cylindrical component of a column.

Ecclesia: In Athens, the Assembly, or legislative body made up of all male citizens.

Elysian Fields: A region of the Underworld reserved for the souls of virtuous people.

Epheboi: The Athenian military training corps.

ephors: "Overseers"; in Sparta, government administrators.

epikleroi: Mainly in Athens, young women without brothers.

episteme: Science.

exedra: An outside sitting/lounging area adjoining the courtyard of a house.

fluting: The vertical grooves carved into most Greek columns.

freedman: A slave who gained his or her freedom.

frieze: A band of sculptures, often running around a Greek temple's perimeter above the colonnade.

genos (plural is gene): A clan.

grammatistes: Teachers of reading, writing, and simple mathematics.

gymnasium: A public facility in which men exercised, played sports, read, and attended lectures.

gymnastiki: Regular exercise.

gynaeceum, or gynaikonitis: The women's quarters of a home.

Hades: The Underworld; the realm of the afterlife.

Hellas: Greece; Hellenes: Greeks.

helots: In Sparta, agricultural serfs exploited and brutalized by Spartan citizens.

Heraia: The women's athletic games held every four years in honor of the goddess Hera.

herm: A bust of the god Hermes placed near the front door of a house to ward off evil.

hetairai: "Companions"; educated women who provided men with sex, entertainment, and conversation.

himation: A loose-fitting garment that wrapped around the body in a variety of styles.

hoplite: An ancient Greek infantry soldier.

hoplon: The shield carried by ancient Greek soldiers.

hybris: Arrogance.

Islands of the Blessed: In the Underworld, a region of eternal happiness reserved for the souls of especially virtuous people.

katagogia: Large hotels.

katakysmata: At a wedding, a ceremonial shower of nuts and sweetmeats.

kerkouroi: Large cargo ships, each equipped with a sail, oars, and a bow ram.

kitharistes: Teachers of music and poetry.

klismos: An armless chair with a wooden back and a seat of cross-hatched leather strips.

knucklebones: A game in which people throw small bones into the air and try to catch them on the backs of their hands.

kratos: Rule or govern.

kykloi: Low platforms used to display goods in a marketplace.

lekythoi: Pottery vases containing liquid offerings for the dead.

liturgy: A system of public contributions to support social activities such as the theater and the erection of statues and monuments.

lyre: A small harp.

metics (metoikoi): In Athens, resident foreigners.

metope: An individual portion, usually square-shaped, of a frieze on a Greek temple.

Minoans: Bronze Age Greeks who inhabited Crete and other Aegean islands.

moikheia: Adultery.

Mycenaeans: Bronze Age Greeks who originally inhabited the Greek mainland and eventually succeeded the Minoans as rulers of the Aegean sphere.

mystery cult: A small, secretive ancient religious sect.

obol: A coin, usually of silver, equal to 1/6 of a drachma.

oikos (plural is oikoi): The family.

oligarchy: "Rule of the few"; a government ruled by a small group of individuals.

Olympians: The Greek gods, who were thought to reside atop Mt. Olympus in the region of Thessaly.

ophthalmia: Redness and swelling of the eyes, a condition common in ancient Greece's dry, dusty climate.

oracle: A temple priestess who was thought to act as a medium between the gods and humans; or the sacred place where a priestess transmitted her divine message; or the message itself.

orchestra: In a Greek theater, the circular stone area in which the actors performed.

order: An architectural style based on the details of the columns employed; the three main Greek orders were the Doric, Ionic, and Corinthian.

ostracism: In Athens, a democratic process in which people voted to banish an unpopular leader.

ostrakon: A pottery fragment on which an Athenian citizen wrote the name of the person he wanted banished.

paidagogos: A slave or freedman hired by parents to accompany a son to school and to supervise his behavior.

paidotribe: A teacher of dancing and athletics.

palaistra: A wrestling school, usually for young boys.

Panathenaea: The large Athenian religious festival held every four years to honor Athens's patron deity, Athena.

pankration: A rough, often brutal combination of wrestling, boxing, and street fighting, popular in public athletic competitions.

pantheon: The group of all the gods worshiped by a people.

parochos: A groom's best man.

pediment: A triangular gable on the front or back end of a Greek temple.

Peloponnesus: The large peninsula that makes up southern Greece.

perioikoi: "Neighbors"; in Sparta, resident foreigners.

petasos: A hat with a low crown and wide brim.

phalanx: A Greek military formation consisting of multiple ranks, with heavily armored hoplites standing or marching side-by-side in each rank.

philo: Love or love of.

phratry: "Blood brotherhood"; an extended kinship group composed of about thirty clans.

phylai: A tribe; in Greece, usually composed of three phratries.

phylarch: The leader of a tribe.

physis: A single and simple underlying principle.

Pnyx: The hill in Athens on which the Assembly met.

polis (plural is poleis): A city-state, or tiny nation built around a central town or city.

portico: A porch, as in the front and rear of a Greek temple.

propylaea: An ornate architectural entranceway, as in the Propylaea of the Athenian Acropolis.

pyx: A woman's makeup case.

quarryman: A worker or supervisor in a stone quarry.

red-figure: A pottery style in which the figures and scenes on the artifacts are reddish-orange against a black background.

River Styx: The river thought to mark the boundary between the world of the living and the Underworld.

sophia: Wisdom or knowledge.

sophist: A teacher who charged money for lessens in public speaking and other subjects.

sophoi: Sages or philosophers.

Spartiates: Spartan citizens; free adult males born into Spartan families.

stoa: A colonnaded, roofed walkway that usually housed shops and offices.

strategoi: In Athens, the ten annually elected military generals.

symposium: A small dinner party, usually in a private home.

talent: A measure of wealth equal to six thousand drachmas in fifth-century B.C. Greece.

Tartarus: A region of the Underworld reserved for the souls of wicked people.

theatron: In a Greek theater, the semicircular seating area.

tholos: A round structure with a conical roof supported by a circular colonnade.

thronos: A large, comfortable chair used by the master of a house.

trapezitai: Bankers and money changers.

triglyph: An ornamental square, containing three vertical shafts, separating one metope from another in a frieze on a Greek temple.

volute: A spiral- or scroll-shaped decoration on the capital of an Ionic column.

For Further Reading

Isaac Asimov, *The Greeks: A Great Adventure*. Boston: Houghton Mifflin, 1965. An excellent, entertaining overview of the ancient Greeks, with an emphasis on their importance to later cultures. Contains some concise explanations of Greek science and philosophy. Written for advanced young readers.

David Bellingham, *An Introduction to Greek Mythology*. Secaucus, NJ: Chartwell Book, 1989. Explains the major Greek myths and legends and their importance to the ancient Greeks. Contains many beautiful photos and drawings.

C. M. Bowra and the Editors of Time-Life Books, *Classical Greece*. New York: Time-Life Books, 1965. This is an excellent, well-rounded presentation of ancient Greek history and culture with many appropriate photos, enhanced by Bowra's keen insights and fine writing style.

Roland and Françoise Etienne, *The Search for Ancient Greece*. New York: Harry N. Abrams, 1992. A detailed but easy-to-read summary of how scholars through the ages discovered and studied the literature, art, and ideas of the classical Greeks. The text is accompanied by many colorful illustrations.

Rhoda A. Hendricks, translator, *Classical Gods and Heroes*. New York: Morrow Quill, 1974. A collection of easy-to-read translations of famous Greek myths and tales, as told by ancient Greek and Roman writers, including Homer, Hesiod, Pindar, Ovid, and Sophocles.

Homer, the *Iliad*, retold by Barbara Leonie Picard. New York: Oxford University Press, 1960; and Homer, the *Odyssey*, retold by Barbara Leonie Picard. New York: Oxford University Press, 1952. Simple, entertaining versions of the epic tales that helped define the classical Greeks' heroic outlook and religious structure. Translated specifically for young readers.

Don Nardo, *Ancient Greece*. San Diego: Lucent Books, 1994; *Greek and Roman Theater*. San Diego: Lucent Books, 1995; and *The Battle of Marathon*. San Diego: Lucent Books, 1996. These concise volumes offer general but essential background information on ancient Greek history, military and social customs, art, literature, and ideas.

Susan Peach and Anne Millard, *The Greeks*. London: Usborne, 1990. A useful general overview of the history, culture, and myths of ancient Greece, written for the basic reader. Filled with excellent and very accurate color illustrations.

Betty Radice, *Who's Who in the Ancient World: A Handbook to the Survivors of the Greek and Roman Classics*. New York: Penguin Books, 1973. A reference that summarizes the important information about the most notable ancient men and women, including the Greeks—Homer, Democritus, Aeschylus, Pericles, Herodotus, Hippocrates, Socrates, Plato, and Aristotle.

Major Works Consulted

C. M. Bowra, *The Greek Experience*. New York: New American Library, 1957. An excellent, penetrating, scholarly discussion of ancient Greek culture and ideas by one of the finest modern classical historians. Highly recommended for those interested in the legacy of Greek thought.

James H. Butler, *The Theater and Drama of Greece and Rome*. San Francisco: Chandler Publishing, 1972. A fine, detailed overview of ancient theater, covering the important playwrights and their works, ancient theaters, play presentation, and audiences. Highly recommended.

Thomas Craven, *The Pocket Book of Greek Art*. New York: Pocket Books, 1950. A well-written discussion of Greek artistic expression, works, and artifacts, with an emphasis on how the creative spirit was an important part of everyday Greek life. The section on sculpture and sculptors is especially good.

Will Durant, *The Life of Greece*. New York: Simon and Schuster, 1966. A detailed, scholarly study of all aspects of Greek civilization, with special emphasis placed on everyday life, social customs, attitudes, and beliefs.

M. I. Finley, *The Ancient Economy*. Berkeley, CA: University of California Press, 1985. In a well-researched volume, Finley presents a fascinating glimpse into the lives and practices of ancient landlords, peasants, merchants, and traders, with useful commentary on land ownership, manufacturing, coinage, money lending, agriculture, and slavery.

———, *Ancient Slavery and Modern Ideology*. New York: Penguin Books, 1980. A very thoughtful and well-written study of all aspects of ancient slavery by a noted classical historian. Finley makes the point that the Greeks, like other ancient peoples, accepted the concept that some people were inferior to others and, therefore, saw slavery as a natural and justifiable institution.

Michael Grant, *The Classical Greeks*. New York: Charles Scribner's Sons, 1989. A collection of short but highly informative biographies of some of the most important figures in Greek history, including artists, playwrights, sculptors, scientists, and philosophers, as well as politicians and military leaders. A very valuable source.

———, *The Rise of the Greeks*. New York: Macmillan, 1987. One of the finest and most prolific of modern classical historians, Grant here delivers a masterful, highly detailed, and scholarly study of Greek civilization, focusing one by one on each important city-state and exploring its founding, development, and contributions.

———, *A Social History of Greece and Rome*. New York: Charles Scribner's Sons, 1992. Another fine book by Grant, this one explores the ins and outs of ancient Greek social life and customs, including the role of women, rich versus poor, and the status of slaves and foreigners.

Charles B. Gulick, *Modern Traits in Old Greek Life*. New York: Cooper Square

Publishers, 1963. This well-organized and well-written volume examines the details of everyday life in ancient Greece. The author supports the information with many pertinent quotes from the historical record; for instance, Socrates' witty remarks about "eating to live" and "living to eat."

Edith Hamilton, *The Greek Way to Western Civilization*. New York: New American Library, 1942. In one of the classic modern studies of the Greeks, Hamilton explores their contributions to the world's art, literature, and philosophy. She explains what made the Greeks unique: their logical and refreshing view of human beings and their place in the scheme of things. A beautifully written, moving, and memorable book.

Herodotus, *The Histories*. Translated by Aubrey de Sélincourt. New York: Penguin Books, 1972. A fine translation of the efforts of the "father of history" in his own words to put "on record the astonishing achievements both of our own and of other peoples; and more particularly, to show how they came into conflict." A priceless source for memorable details about ancient Greek culture and attitudes.

Peter James and Nick Thorpe, *Ancient Inventions*. New York: Ballantine Books, 1994. A fasinating study of the "who," "when," and "how" of thousands of everyday utensils, tools, weapons, personal belongings, foods, public institutions, habits, and ideas introduced by the ancients, including the Greeks.

Ian Jenkins, *Greek and Roman Life*. Cambridge, MA: Harvard University Press, 1986. This book was compiled to accompany an exhibit by the British Museum about daily life in ancient Greece and Rome. Though short (just seventy pages), it is very well written and contains much useful information, as well as numerous excellent illustrations and photos. Highly recommended.

Pierre Léveque, *The Birth of Greece*. New York: Harry N. Abrams, 1994. A commendable introduction to ancient Greek history and culture, with insightful commentary, and filled with first-rate photos, drawings, reproductions of paintings and sculptures, and re-creations of temples and other buildings in their original form. Highly recommended.

John Miliadis, *The Acropolis*. Athens: M. Pechlivanidis, no date given. A useful description of the renowned "high point of the city" on which the Greeks built some of the most beautiful buildings of all times. Includes background information on how the various structures were constructed, maps, ground plans, and many photos.

John Peradotto and J. P. Sullivan, eds., *Women in the Ancient World: The Arethusa Papers*. Albany, NY: State University of Albany Press, 1984. A useful collection of scholarly articles and essays on the subject, including such titles as "Early Greece: The Origins of the Western Attitude Toward Women," "Classical Greek Attitudes to Sexual Behavior," and "Plato: Misogynist, Phaedophile, and Feminist."

Plutarch, *Lives of the Noble Grecians and Romans*, excerpted in *The Rise and Fall of Athens: Nine Greek Lives*. Translated by Ian Scott-Kilvert. New York: Penguin Books, 1960. This useful volume contains clear, easy-to-read translations of nine of the ancient writer's famous biographies, including those of Solon, the lawgiver; Cimon, the empire builder; and Alcibiades, the traitor.

Marjorie Quennell and C. H. B. Quennell, *Everyday Things in Ancient Greece*. New York: G. P. Putnam's Sons, 1954. The Quennells, thorough and thoughtful scholars, present a detailed and enlightening discussion of Greek culture, customs, and ideas while citing the literary and archaeological sources for this knowledge.

Charles Alexander Robinson Jr., *Athens in the Age of Pericles*. Norman: University of Oklahoma Press, 1959. A detailed look at everyday life in Athens during Greece's golden age, with plenty of discussion of Greek democracy and politics, as well as descriptions of art, drama, and sculpture.

C. E. Robinson, *Everyday Life in Ancient Greece*. Oxford, England: Clarendon Press, 1968. An insightful examination of ancient Greek life, with well-developed discussions of the heroic age, the rise of city-states, Sparta's peculiar customs, Athenian democracy, and the roles of women and slaves.

Leonard Whibley, ed., *A Companion to Greek Studies*. New York: Hafner Publishing, 1963. This massive (763 pages) volume contains a wealth of information on ancient Greek history, ethnology, warfare, literature, art, architecture, philosophy, customs, and institutions. Each section is presented by a different and distinguished historian. Highly technical in nature, this is not meant as leisurely reading, but rather, as a reference work to provide background material for more specific readings and studies. Highly recommended.

Additional Works Consulted

James T. Allen, *Stage Antiquities of the Greeks and Romans and Their Influence.* New York: Cooper Square Publishers, 1963.

Reginald E. Allen, ed., *Greek Philosophy: Thales to Aristotle.* New York: Macmillan, 1985.

W. H. Auden, ed., *The Portable Greek Reader.* New York: Viking Press, 1948.

H. C. Baldry, *The Greek Tragic Theater.* New York: W. W. Norton, 1971.

John Boardman, *Greek Art.* New York: Thames and Hudson, 1985.

J. Burnet, ed., *Early Greek Philosophy.* London: A. and C. Black, 1930.

Lionel Casson, ed., *Masters of Ancient Comedy.* New York: Macmillan, 1960.

Rodney Castleden, *Minoans: Life in Bronze Age Crete.* New York: Routledge, 1990.

Robert B. Downs, *Books That Changed the World.* New York: Penguin Books, 1983.

H. C. Evelyn-White, trans., *The Works of Hesiod.* Cambridge, MA: Harvard University Press, 1914.

Elaine Fantham et al., *Women in the Classical World.* New York: Oxford University Press, 1994.

M. I. Finley, *The Ancient Greeks.* New York: Penguin Books, 1977.

W. G. Forrest, *The Emergence of Greek Democracy: The Character of Greek Politics, 800–400 B.C.* London: Weidenfeld and Nicolson, 1966.

———, *A History of Sparta, 950–192 B.C.* New York: W. W. Norton, 1968.

Hartvig Frisch, trans., *The Constitution of the Athenians.* Copenhagen: Nordisk Forlag, 1952.

Michael Grant, *The Ancient Mediterranean.* New York: Penguin Books, 1969.

———, *The Founders of the Western World: A History of Greece and Rome.* New York: Charles Scribner's Sons, 1991.

———, *The Myths of the Greeks and Romans.* New York: Penguin Books, 1962.

Peter Green, *The Parthenon.* New York: Newsweek Book Division, 1973.

Moses Hadas, ed., *The Complete Plays of Aristophanes.* New York: Bantam Books, 1962.

Edith Hamilton, *Mythology.* New York: New American Library, 1940.

Victor Davis Hanson, *The Western Way of War: Infantry Battle in Classical Greece.* New York: Oxford University Press, 1989.

W. G. Hardy, *The Greek and Roman World.* Cambridge, MA: Schenkman, 1962.

Sally C. Humphreys, *The Family, Women, and Death: Comparative Studies.* London: Routledge and Kegan Paul, 1983.

Robert M. Hutchins, ed., *The Works of Aristotle.* Chicago: Encyclopaedia Britannica, 1952.

Peter Jay, ed., *The Greek Anthology and Other Ancient Epigrams.* New York: Penguin Books, 1981.

C. Kerenyi, *The Gods of the Greeks.* New York: Thames and Hudson, 1951.

H. D. F. Kitto, *The Greeks*. Baltimore: Penguin Books, 1951.

Bernard Knox, ed., *The Norton Book of Classical Literature*. New York: W. W. Norton, 1993.

Richard Lattimore, trans., *Greek Lyrics*. Chicago: University Chicago Press, 1960.

———, *The Odes of Pindar*. Chicago: University of Chicago Press, 1976.

Peter Levi, *Atlas of the Greek World*. New York: Facts On File, 1984.

Lysias, *Speeches*. Translated by W. R. M. Lamb. Cambridge, MA: Harvard University Press, 1930.

E. C. Marchant et al., trans., *Xenophon in Seven Volumes*. Cambridge, MA: Harvard University Press, 1921.

Gilbert Murray, *The Literature of Ancient Greece*. Chicago: University of Chicago Press, 1956.

Cornelius Nepos, *The Book of the Great Generals of Foreign Nations*. Translated by John C. Rolfe. Cambridge, MA: Harvard University Press, 1960.

Whitney J. Oates and Eugene O'Neill Jr., eds., *The Complete Greek Drama*. New York: Random House, 1938.

Robert Payne, *Ancient Greece: The Triumph of a Culture*. New York: W. W. Norton, 1964.

Plato, *Dialogues*. Translated by Benjamin Jowett. New York: Random House, 1937.

———, *The Republic*. Translated by F.M. Cornford. New York: Oxford University Press, 1945.

———, *Symposium*. Translated by Tom Griffith. Berkeley: University of California Press, 1989.

Plutarch, *The Lives of the Noble Grecians and Romans*. Translated by John Dryden. Chicago: Encyclopaedia Britannica, 1952.

Jane Polley, ed., *Quest for the Past*. Pleasantville, NY: Reader's Digest Association, 1984.

Meyer Reinhold, *Essentials of Greek and Roman Classics: A Guide to the Humanities*. Great Neck, NY: Barron's Educational Series, 1946.

Paul Roche, trans., *The Orestes Plays of Aeschylus*. New York: New American Library, 1962.

W. D. Ross, ed., *The Works of Aristotle*. Oxford, England: Clarendon Press, 1921.

Chester G. Starr, *The Ancient Greeks*. New York: Oxford University Press, 1971.

Joseph J. Thorndike Jr., ed., *Mysteries of the Past*. New York: American Heritage, 1977.

Thucydides, *The Peloponnesian Wars*. First published ca. 400 B.C. Modern edition translated by Benjamin Jowett. New York: Washington Square Press, 1963.

Charles Van Doren, *A History of Knowledge: Past, Present, and Future*. New York: Ballantine Books, 1991.

Index

Picture Credits

About the Author

Don Nardo is an award-winning author whose more than seventy books cover a wide range of topics. He has produced more than thirty historical volumes, including studies of five of America's wars; a political trilogy consisting of *Democracy*, *The U.S. Congress*, and *The U.S. Presidency*; an examination of the struggles of African Americans in colonial times entitled *Braving the New World*; and biographies of Thomas Jefferson, Franklin D. Roosevelt, William Lloyd Garrison, and H. G. Wells. Mr. Nardo's specialty is the ancient world, about which he has written *The Roman Republic, The Roman Empire, The Punic Wars, Caesar's Conquest of Gaul, The Battle of Zama, Traditional Japan*, and biographies of Cleopatra and Julius Caesar. Mr. Nardo has also written numerous screenplays and teleplays, including works for Warner Brothers and ABC Television. He lives with his wife, Christine, on Cape Cod, Massachusetts.